Foreign-Language Study

Foreign-Language Study

Perspective and Prospect

Roger A. Pillet

The University of Chicago Press
Chicago and London

The University of Chicago Press, Chicago 60637
The University of Chicago Press, Ltd., London
© 1974 by The University of Chicago
All rights reserved. Published 1974
Printed in the United States of America
International Standard Book Number: 0-226-66826-6
Library of Congress Catalog Card Number: 73-84194

Roger A. Pillet is a professor in
the Graduate School of Education of
The University of Chicago. Among
his many publications is *French in
the Elementary School* (with Harold
B. Dunkel).
[1974]

To Etiennette
constructive critic
unflagging coworker
gifted teacher
inspiring wife

Contents

Introduction

Perhaps the most impressive product of the ferment in the foreign-language field in the last two decades is the exhaustive literature now available to those interested in the subject. The writing of another volume to be added to the already loaded foreign-language shelf may seem a mere display of knowledge or it may reflect a presumptuous notion that the literature available is less informative and substantial than it might be. I should like to think that neither of these attitudes apply, that there are legitimate justifications for an analytic overview of language learning and teaching in the United States to this day.

The foreign-language situation in the 1970s is markedly different from that which prevailed in the past two decades: from the point of view of national climate, financial support, acceptance of foreign languages in the total curriculum, enrollment, and teacher employment, the profession has arrived at a decision point.

It is my intention to review briefly each of these areas in the hope that a careful analysis of the past may suggest viable alternatives for future courses of action.

Additionally, there is ample evidence that, in the current decade, there is need to develop a new philosophy, to reconsider new or modified objectives, to explore new methodologies, to modify radically our teaching strategies and our course content if foreign languages are to survive as a consequential part of the general pattern of formal education.

In the first part of the study, I shall outline the historical forces contributing to resurgent interest in foreign-language instruction after World War II and attempt to assess the degree to which each contributed in some significant way to the momentum that characterizes the field in the past decade. At the same time, I shall attempt to explain how a number of elements in the total foreign-language configuration fell short of expectations, or were insufficiently exploited, or were simply ineffectual. I shall rely heavily on documentation to supplement my own limited expertise in many of the areas discussed. Faced either with imposing my references on all readers or with making elaborations optional, I have chosen the second alternative: my text reflects only broad lines of discussion but adequate references are available to those wishing to pursue their own investigation in greater depth.

In the second part I shall attempt to elaborate my own notions of what constitutes an effective base line for improved instruction in the present and near future and to suggest ways in which a renewed total professional effort might contribute to a massive impact on foreign languages as a revitalized and essential part of modern curriculum.

It is hoped that the following pages, insofar as they reflect the thoughts and theories of many gifted and dedicated individuals, will leave a general impression with the reader that the foreign-language profession can look with pride on its past accomplishments. It is hoped that, in different degrees, various sections of this essay will bring helpful perceptions to administrators, to teachers at all levels and in all subjects, and, more specifically, to those experienced teachers or those preparing to teach who are committed to transmit their attitude and their knowledge to new generations of students looking to our schools for productive and provocative intellectual experiences.

Acknowledgements

Finally, a word of thanks to the numerous colleagues and countless students who, over two decades, have shaped the experience reflected in the following pages.

I should also like to give due credit to Nancy Baum for her assistance in preparing the footnotes and the final manuscript.

More particularly, I should like to express my gratitude to Harold B. Dunkel for his careful reading of the manuscript, for his perceptive comments, and for his continuing professional and personal support over the past years.

Part One

Perspective

1   Transition

Historical Perspective

The teaching of foreign languages in the United States has a long
and continuous history.[1] We are told, for instance, of the zeal of
missionaries, as early as 1604, to impart some knowledge of the
French language to the Indians among whom they were working,
primarily as a means of exposing them to religious doctrine. By
1700, schools and seminaries concerned not only with instruction
of Indians but also with the teaching of children of immigrants
were in operation from eastern Canada to the Gulf of Mexico.

    Another agency interested in the teaching of foreign language
"with a view of its usefulness both to commerce and general
education" was the colonial private school. We find that in the
early 1700s French was being taught, basically for the purpose of
instructing children of émigrés, in New York and in South
Carolina. Private instruction in French was available in Boston.
Philadelphia and Virginia also are listed as places where
instruction in French was offered.

    The teaching of foreign languages was, therefore, fairly
extensive through private tutorial system or in denominational
schools by the late 1800s. There is evidence that teaching, in spite
of often picturesque and perhaps exaggerated claims, was spotty
and that the result in terms of language competence was often less
than spectacular.

    It is difficult in reviewing the statements available on the
subject to determine exactly for what age level some of this
instruction was intended. We assume that in many cases the study
of French was extended down to children of elementary school
age. There is a record, however, that a certain William Clajon
indicated in 1761 that he would not take children and that he

would undertake "to teach no others but such as willing and capable of improvement," for he was determined "not to sacrifice his honor and character either to the caprices of children or to the lavishness of some parent" (Watts, "The Teaching of French," p. 23).

Gradually, public schools as well as private schools offered foreign-language instruction in a more formal way. Generally, these institutions were committed to a classical orientation that, in terms of language teaching, involved Latin and Greek. The introduction of modern languages as part of the curriculum was slow. German was added in the Philadelphia schools in 1800 and French added soon after. French was part of the curriculum in the New York School in 1830 and certain private institutions such as Andover, Amherst, and Mount Holyoke are on record as offering French beginning about 1830. It may be noted, however, that in many instances the foreign language was considered a kind of cocurricular activity, listed among special studies that, in some cases, involved extra fees.

By 1900 there was a strong movement in the Catholic elementary schools, particularly those of Louisiana and New England, to continue with the teaching of foreign languages. This was paralleled by the teaching of German in a number of denominational schools. Surprisingly, the record indicates that in 1895 some 3,000 students were enrolled in French classes in contrast to some 23,000 youngsters involved in German. By 1900, frequent recommendations were made to make elementary foreign-language instruction optional at the lower school level but eventually, during World War I, the passage of laws hostile to foreign-language instruction in twenty-three states further reduced the thrust for foreign-language instruction prior to the university level.

This brief overview is intended to indicate that, until recent times, interest in systematic study of foreign languages (particularly the modern ones) was sporadic and capricious, often influenced by ethnic and political considerations. Before World War II, foreign-language offerings were negligible prior to the university where, by 1940, instruction had become relatively uniform with respect to goals and practices.

In institutions of higher learning the study of foreign languages was increasingly considered prerequisite to humanistic studies. In 1929, the Coleman Report,[2] though not universally accepted by the profession, recommended emphasis on reading as the skill most achievable given the constraint of time resulting from competition of various subject matters in the curriculum. Reading was also considered the most useful skill insofar as it provided the tool needed to unlock the treasures of the rich literary heritage of the respective languages.

Those in the foreign-language profession who disagreed with the report could, at that time at least, adduce very little evidence that development of conversational skills was important enough to justify the investment of many additional hours of exposure. Furthermore, in spite of the broad and progressive notions on foreign-language study expressed by Sweet, Jespersen, and Palmer, the profession as a whole was ill prepared to implement in a substantial way a more effective program for acquiring the time-consuming skills of understanding and speaking.[3] The academic trend met no organized resistance from the public, which generally saw little relevance between foreign-language instruction and social conditions and were little concerned with verbal communication as a means of international rapprochement. As a matter of fact, many communities were deliberately intent on eroding linguistic and cultural ties with the foreign countries of their respective origins.[4]

The "art" of reading was systematically developed to a high level of efficiency around the time of the Coleman Report.[5] Decoding of the printed message involved the assimilations of an incremental lexical repertoire and an "understanding" of grammar that could provide the morphological and syntactical signals necessary to coherent "inductive reading." For this purpose a number of frequency lists were compiled,[6] a number of reference grammars became "standard" over several generations,[7] and major works dealing with methodology attested to the continuing interest in structuring viable programs.[8]

Since the period seemed to have reached relative consensus as to goals, method, and, to a great extent, materials, the teacher's preparation and the teacher's task were relatively clear-cut. His or her preparation involved the achievement of expertise in literature, the reading of which was the ultimate objective of skill development, and the following of fairly clear-cut directions to achieve such reading competency as would lead to a sensitive reading of the literature.

Perhaps even more significant as contributing to the instructor's equanimity was the fact that he was usually dealing with an academically talented student population consisting only of those who had demonstrated intellectual capacity in the high school and were committed to meeting the challenge of higher education. Many among that group had chosen to pursue foreign-language study as a matter of intrinsic motivation or as preparation to becoming foreign-language teachers.

In recent times, the configuration outlined above has been castigated as characteristic of an "elitist" concept of education. Tensions have indeed been raised as a result of influx into colleges of a number of students wishing to continue in spite of insufficient or inappropriate early instruction. Without, at this point, arguing the merits or demerits of the situation, let us indicate that, in earlier times, the elitist concept was subscribed to by both teachers and students, the former willing to exercise their function as "selectors," the latter willing to accept the teacher's evaluation as a constructive measure of potential for mastery of the subject in question. The fact that in many cases existing "requirements" complicated the general mutuality of agreement on goals and procedures argues more for removal of requirements than for a readjustment of the system.

Nor can one forget that focusing on "trends" tends to distort the total picture. In the heyday of the reading objective many teachers, concerned with the value of students' mastering at least minimal conversational skills, provided additional opportunity for manipulating linguistic items within the context of the grammar-translation method.[9] Even in that period many students, as a result of "manipulative exercises" practiced to the point of automaticity, emerged with excellent competence in the conversational skills.

It is equally important to note that during the whole of the grammar-translation period a variety of "direct method" exponents was championing the cause of conversational skills. Needless to say, then as now and regardless of the basic method prevailing, results were dependent in great part on the quality of the teaching, the teacher's ability to "get through" to the student, to make the subject live and to motivate the class.[10]

Transition to the "New Key"

Although, in retrospect, the turning point in the reorientation of foreign-language studies is generally attributed to the launching of Sputnik, that event merely served to dramatize concrete, significant changes that had been gestating during the previous ten years, particularly in connection with the Army Specialized Training Programs. The deployment of Armed Forces personnel in many countries of the globe during World War II made it evident that American soldiers and officers abroad were usually unable to cope, even at a minimal linguistic level, with situations involving their own safety and the successful conduct of military operations. In response to this very real crisis and as an extension of its own facilities, the Armed Forces contracted a number of crash programs to educational institutions. Because of the completely utilitarian purpose of these programs they can be characterized by a number of common features.[11]

The programs were designed to be functional: since inability to communicate verbally in the foreign land was seen as the greatest impediment to field operations abroad, development of the understanding and speaking skills became the primary, if not sole objective, of instruction. The parameter of instruction was limited: ability to communicate in a restricted number of predictable situations suggested narrowly circumscribed lexical and structural loading of the content. Because of the urgency of the national need, the programs were intensive, involving some six-hundred contact hours compressed in twelve to fifteen weeks of instruction. Since spontaneity of expression was seen as contributing to effective communication, the method was predicated on the theory of overlearning to the point where, to approximate native control, the stimulus-response process became automatic. The latter implied intensive drill on vocabulary embedded in structures, usually modeled by native informants with provision for additional practice facilitated by records and films. Last, given the worldwide deployment of American troops, the programs extended beyond the modern foreign languages traditionally taught in our schools. Provisions were made for the teaching of such "exotic" languages as Chinese, Japanese, and so on.

It is to be noted that the army programs, in addition to refocusing the goals of foreign-language instruction, reflect a convergence of resources instrumental in meeting these goals. Linguists, basically committed to the primacy of the spoken word, contributed a methodology that enhanced mastery of language as spoken communication. The need for a tireless drillmaster instrumental in overlearning pointed to the practicality of electronic aids as efficient extensions of the teacher. Recordings also provided a variety of models facilitating the task and extending the role of the native informant.

The fact that the army programs were publicized as successful helped to sustain interest in the basic approach even after the cessation of military hostilities. Because universities had been involved as subcontractors in the program transposition of the method into the peacetime classroom was facilitated. *An Investigation of Second Language Learning* by Agard and Dunkel in 1948[12] addresses itself to the evaluation of the positive and negative features of the "army method" as continued in some forty-eight institutions after the war, particularly with respect to the problem of "transferability" of the new method to civilian classrooms. This and a companion book, *Second Language Learning*,[13] constitute a call for more rigor in determining goals and evaluating results in the area of foreign-language instruction and for serious reassessment of complex factors interacting in the foreign-language class. As a follow-up to these studies the Chicago Language Conference brought a number of distinguished foreign-language educators to the University of

Chicago in 1948 with the purpose of translating the Agard-Dunkel findings into practice.[14] Because the recommendations of two working committees instituted by the conference reflect the commitment to and direction of the Modern Language Association, and since these common views express the tenor of the period, we shall summarize them in some detail.[15]

A number of recommendations addressed themselves to the study of the role of foreign languages in the total curriculum. Surveys were to be conducted to determine the role of language in general education, the existing professional outlets for foreign languages, and the possibilities of using the foreign languages in schools through interdisciplinary cooperative efforts. Particular emphasis was placed on the possibilities of transfer in language learning and the integration thereof with pupil activity in other disciplines. The organization of pupil activities in the language class for better motivation and more effective practice was considered important since use of the language in some form is justification for language learning.

In addition to overriding questions involving usage, concern was expressed for clearer definition on the nature of language, including a clearer notion of what achievement could be expected in the respective skills. This, in turn, led to questions relating to specific objectives as appropriate to various levels of instruction in terms of individual and societal needs, to the development of criteria for the selection of students, and to the need for articulating instruction as students passed from one level to another.

Important additional recommendations involved the preparation of materials suitable for the secondary school that were based on careful descriptive linguistic analysis, particularly of the auditory type, which at the same time would narrow the gap between the conversational approach and the existing reading materials. Frequency lists reflecting spontaneous colloquial speech in respect to syntax and idioms as well as vocabulary were to be compiled. The development of audiovisual aids, especially the sound film, was endorsed as contributing to more effective teaching and a complete repertoire of testing techniques and materials was to be provided to measure all of the above objectives.

A great deal of emphasis was placed on the research function. Controlled experimentation was to be conducted to determine the results obtained from large amounts of contact hours in an intensive program, to cast light on the problems of satiety and the rate of forgetting and to determine the relationship of oral-aural instruction to reading efficiency.

By means of studying old and new experimental courses some determination would be made as to what was proper teaching for ear-minded as well as eye-minded students. Last, a strong recommendation was made for the establishment of a service for the collection and distribution of information on language-teaching projects, materials, and work in progress. The committees were well aware that, assuming some degree of success in meeting their ambitious goals, a massive effort would be needed to retrain teachers capable of implementing a new system of instruction.

The ambitious projections outlined above might well have remained a pious hope without the financial assistance necessary to convert aspirations into effective action. Fortunately, the conviction that a radical new orientation would make for more general and more effective language teaching came at a propitious time. Various aspects of the new aural-oral (eventually audio-lingual) approach were popularized under the heading of teaching in the "New Key."[16] Proponents of the method were encouraged by substantial financial support and by a national climate conducive to encouraging the study of foreign languages.

The Modern Language Association, under the forceful leadership of William Riley Parker whose tenure as secretary began in 1947, was responsible for systematically planning programs that would lead to more extensive and improved foreign-language instruction.[17] Initially supported by grants from the Rockefeller Foundation (1952-58), the association did much to reverse the trends that, in previous years, had eroded the status of foreign languages in the eye of the public and in the schools. On a more positive side, it specified directions for new materials and new strategies that would make foreign languages more productive for a wider range of students at all levels of instruction.

The urgent revision in content and method exemplified in the "New Key" was consonant with a national concern extending to other disciplines, particularly mathematics and sciences. In 1963, James B. Conant, while concerned principally with the training of teachers, attributed the "lag" of American education on the international scene to previous lack of emphasis on "hard," traditional subjects and recommended a return to stringent subject-matter requirements as an imperative for the survival of American schools. Since foreign languages fell in the category of traditional subjects, the influence of Conant's position tended to minimize resistance to foreign-language instruction in the academic arena.[18]

Scattered support (perhaps unexpected) from officialdom provided further encouragement to the language profession: Earl J. McGrath, the Commissioner of Education, endorsed foreign language as important to general education in 1952;[19] in 1953 Oliver J. Caldwell, then assistant commissioner in the Office of Education, subscribed to the importance of teaching foreign languages at as early an age as was practical.[20] The launching of Sputnik in 1957 dramatically confirmed the academic and official position that improved instruction was essential in dominating international competition and vital to national survival and welfare.

It was in this climate, resulting from a convergence of political social, and pedagogical forces, that the National Defense Education Act was passed and signed in 1958.

The "New Key" Is a Golden Key

The Office of Education, which was responsible for the dispensing of funds made available through NDEA, was committed to the proposition that competence in foreign languages could bolster the national defense and was specific in outlining activities appropriate to this purpose. In a modern world where technology had shrunk distances to the point that transportation and communication systems were making even remotely situated countries proximate to the American scene, the prevailing monolingual American attitude seriously impeded our participation in politics, business, and social intercourse. In a world seemingly desperate to enter an era of international rapport, greater insights into foreign cultures were needed by our citizenry if the image of the monocultural American was to be revised and if the harmony necessary to the vision of world peace was to become a reality. In other words, programs supported under NDEA would be consonant with an extension of the principles that had girded the army programs and that MLA had supported as salutary to the foreign-language area. Ability to communicate verbally and to be more objective about cultural gaps were essential objectives.

There was one substantial difference, however. The scope of the programs was to be expanded: it was no longer a question of preparing a relatively few members of the military; a new massive effort was directed at dramatically raising the foreign-language "quotient" of the entire population.

The Office of Education was realistically prepared to support this ambitious goal by providing the substantial financial support required to insure implementation. The seriousness of the government's commitment is documented by a comparison of proposed federal funding with Modern Language Association projections. Whereas the MLA had planned for expenditures of some 5.5 million to cover a five-year plan, NDEA support involved some 135 million for the same period of time. Chart 1 illustrates the comparison in some detail.[21]

Systematic effort to revitalize foreign-language instruction was directed at four major areas. Though these areas sometimes (and necessarily) overlapped, I shall outline them summarily at present and discuss each in greater detail in later pages.

It was wisely decided that embarking on the programs of the magnitude projected made it imperative to collect such data as would be essential to judicious decisions in setting priorities for eventual appropriations. The profession needed to know where it has been, where it was, and what seemed the best alternatives for new directions. Consequently, a number of surveys were subsidized dealing with such varied topics as the history of teaching a number of popular languages in the Unites States, enrollment,

CHART 1

MLA Plan	*NDEA Five-Year Achievement*
Expenditure: $5,425,000	$135,000,000
Institutes: 15 for 900 teachers	300 for 15,000 teachers
Fellowships for secondary school teachers:500	0
Fellowships for potential college teachers: 0	3,450 (Title VI)
Grants for foreign travel for in-service teachers: 250	0
Contract teaching materials for uncommon languages: "several"	120
Language and area centers established: 0	55
Tests: 7 areas for 6 languages	7 areas for 5 languages
State supervisory services, 3 states for 2 years, 47 states for 1 year	38 states
Demonstration centers: 15	0

teacher availability and qualifications, current instructional practices, requirements for students and teacher trainees, lists of available and recommended materials, and so on.[22]

Second, given the commitment to a different set of objectives to be attained through a radically new methodology, substantial support was given for the development, evaluation, and dissemination of audio-lingual materials that would bring the "New Key" approach into the classroom at all levels of instruction. The "Glastonbury Materials" are typical of this effort. Devised by a group composed of language scholars, linguists, psychologists, and practitioners, the materials represent a team approach to the effective implementation of audio-lingual philosophy. Eventually appearing on the commercial market under the rubric of *A-LM Materials* (Harcourt, Brace and World, 1961), they were the first to provide for a four-year sequence (in French, German, Italian, Spanish, and Russian) and eventually to set a pattern for other competitive commercial packages.[23]

In the meantime, substantial investments were made to develop textbooks, grammars, readers, and lexicons as tools in the teaching of "exotic" languages, those almost completely neglected in the general curriculum of this country up to the Second World War.[24]

It is to be noted that recordings, tapes, and a variety of visual aids were considered as an integral part of the audio-lingual system. As a consequence, funding was made available not only for the development of multimedia materials but also for the purchase of these materials and for the acquisition of the machines that they necessitated, including relatively expensive language-laboratory systems.[25]

Third, a major investment was made in the area of teacher preparation. The justification for this expenditure is self-apparent. The desire to make foreign languages accessible to *all* suggested a vast increase in enrollment with a consequent shortage of qualified teachers. It was not only the college population that was expected to increase because of a greater percentage of college-bound students. Popularization of foreign-language study combined with the population explosion was also to swell the number of students in foreign-language classes in secondary schools. The introduction of foreign languages in the elementary school (FLES), consistent with the tenor of the time and sweeping the country in the late 50s, created problems not so much because more teachers would be needed but because teachers in the FLES category would need a radically different orientation.

The essential problem was not purely a numerical one. Such teachers as were available and those yet to be trained had to be conversant with the new objectives and capable of applying the audio-lingual method in class. Furthermore, the new approach called for demonstrating and using conversational skills as an essential part of the teaching strategy. Many teachers (old and new) emerging from "traditional" preparation found themselves insufficiently prepared in aural-oral skills. In addition, many had not been prepared through personal experience or course work to cope with the cultural and linguistic dimensions associated with the "New Key."

In response, a massive program of institutes, at home and abroad, were organized to "retread" experienced teachers.[26] Preservice academic programs geared to the "New Key" were heavily subsidized through fellowship grants.[27] Language and area centers were established and state supervisors were appointed to monitor instruction and improve practices through visitations and workshops.[28]

Last, provisions were made for evaluation at several levels. Guidelines and criteria reflecting professional consensus were drawn for determining the competence of teachers[29] and institutions[30] involved in the foreign-language learning and teaching process. Specific tests were devised to measure competence levels in the various skills.[31] Major projects were periodically funded for assessing the effectiveness of methodology and instructional media.[32] Money was allocated for studies involving "pure" research in the fields of psychology and linguistics, particularly as these sciences related to improved instruction.[33]

Grants were also made to subcontractors with a view to monitoring the effectiveness of the Office of Education's overall program as well as its component parts.

I might add, parenthetically, a more subtle yet significant way in which the study of foreign languages was supported: a number of monographs addressed to students, counselors, and teachers tried to popularize foreign-language study by pointing out the needs and outlets for such studies.[34]

This kind of stimulation was bound to provide a powerful catalyst, to revitalize interest in the foreign-language field.

2   Retrospect

Positive Thrust

For those who, out of disenchantment, tend to minimize the impact of the last two decades as well as for those who have not had opportunity to be aware of activities in the foreign-language field, I shall sketch, by contrasting the then and now, some of the major contributions emerging from the well-supported programs previously described. It is to be noted that, in many cases, the profession has assumed responsibility for continuance and expansion even after the discontinuation of federal support.

I am not concerned with a detailed analysis or with an impartial assessment as a form of academic exercise. I am primarily intent on providing the new teacher and others interested in the educational enterprise with an inventory of the resources now available as a result of the activities of the last decade. I feel that the practitioner of today should be aware of the problems that have been raised, those that have been solved, as well as those that remain perplexing, since such scrutiny leads to better understanding of what needs to be done or reconsidered in the current period.

The most unequivocal, permanent, and promising achievement may be the vast body of literature accumulated and disseminated to the profession in the last generation. The Office of Education's initial thrust in the direction of information gathering has paid off handsomely. The voluminous literature now available reflects development of a professional identity and of constructive, aggressive concern for pedagogical aspirations.

Professional organizations not only grew in membership but provided increasingly meaningful forums for those members attending regularly scheduled meetings.[1] Professional journals published by the respective organizations reflect improved quality, increased sophistication, and a commitment to systematic planning.[2] Periodic conferences at the regional and national level were organized, which were instrumental in setting policy or clarifying issues.[3]

A number of conferences came to be held regularly (the Northeast Conference, for instance) and have since proliferated.[4] Under the auspices of parent organizations national committees have functioned on a regular basis (e.g., the FLES Committee of the AATF). The resulting regularly published reports record a variety of discussions vital and appropriate to the passing scene.[5]

The newly appointed state offices of foreign-language supervisors have been tireless in the organizing of local workshops through which theory and models for improved practices were disseminated at the grass roots level.[6] Recently (1966), the American Council of Teachers of Foreign Languages emerged as a viable, energetic organization, an additional agency for coordinating the energies of the total profession.[7]

A few illustrations will suffice to demonstrate how information and general resources increased in a relatively few years.

In contrast to the fragmentary bibliographies published here and there in the periodicals around 1955, the teacher and researcher now has access to a data bank provided by the ERIC Center for foreign languages.[8]

The FLES teacher, once dependent on Andersson's book and on testimonials and anecdotes in the MLA Newsletter, a main source of support and direction, can now become conversant with the field through Mildred Donoghue's comprehensive *Foreign Languages and the Elementary School Child*.[9] In 1961, Nelson Brooks' *Foreign Languages: Theory and Practice* was, by default, the cornerstone of "New Key" philosophy and one of the few source books available for transforming ideas into classroom practices. His work was soon supplemented by Lado's *Language Testing* (1961) and *Language Teaching* (1964). Since then, numerous handbooks have appeared (Michel, Grittner, Valdman, Politzer, Huebener, Rivers, and Chastain)[10] dealing with general pedagogical guidance, while others have addressed

themselves to more specific related areas: Hocking to the
laboratory[11] and Valette to test construction,[12] for example.

Most useful as a culmination of this avalanche of information
is the recently available *Britannica Review of Foreign Language
Education.*[13] The value of this compendium cannot be under-
estimated. Carefully organized to speak to the various disciplines and factors affecting foreign-language learning and
teaching, it not only provides a cogent discussion of each area but
documents each discussion by means of an extensive bibliography at the end of each section. Because it provides initial
direction and facilitates further investigation in depth, the book is
an invaluable tool for teachers and teacher-trainees, scholars, and
practitioners.

I underline the significance of the above resources. For,
whatever problems beset foreign-language instruction at this
time, an effective machinery and almost limitless information is
available and instrumental in identifying, analyzing, and solving
these problems.

FLES: An Exemplar

I shall eventually return to a detailed discussion of the status of
different aspects of related disciplines and operational factors
as they have developed under the aegis of the "New Key" and as
they suggest direction for the future.

But first, let us consider the history of FLES as central to the
identification of the problems alluded to above. For the FLES
movement is inseparably integrated in the fabric of the audio-
lingual method, and FLES, now at its nadir, may well illuminate the positive and negative forces affecting the total foreign-
language picture.

Although FLES was not new and, as a matter of fact, had been
implemented successfully and studied seriously in Cleveland in
the 1930s,[14] it could not be considered, in 1955, a serious
contender for inclusion in the already crowded elementary
curriculum. The negative attitude of the public toward foreign-
language study, our past tradition of isolation, administrators'
typical lack of sympathy for foreign-language study and their

understandable reluctance to divert funds into a new and untested area, the fact that developing language skills was not particularly consonant with prevailing trends to nurture the "whole" child in terms of meaningful, experiential academic activities directly related to his development as a productive citizen—all of these considerations, combined in various proportions, should have militated against the opportunity to introduce FLES in the schools.[15]

Yet it not only was introduced in many "experimental" programs but, for several years, seemed destined to become a permanent and essential part of the elementary curriculum.[16] Though select programs are still thriving, the period of expansion has been over for several years. Many programs have been discontinued and most still in operation are located in the upper grades, a grudging extension of foreign-language instruction rather than a new movement with its permanent base in the third or fourth grade.

Public pressure was in great part responsible for the initiation and multiplication of FLES programs. Parent groups, elated by the national defense argument, subscribed to the proposition that, as future citizens of a "rapidly shrinking world," their children should eventually become competent to communicate with people of other lands. Obviously, this would not be achieved through the type of instruction to which the older generation had been exposed, the kind of preparation that enabled you to read but left you helpless in a face-to-face encounter with speakers of another language. Parents may not have had a clear idea of the aural-oral approach, but they were convinced that it was bound to be far superior to what they remembered of their own training.

The professionals, the "architects" of FLES, were ready with a substantial rationale to undergird and enhance the public's commitment. For if, they too professed, the grammar-translation method had produced very narrow achievement for a small and select population, the audio-lingual approach (on the parallel that it approximated the "natural" method) was achievable by all students exposed to it regardless of the student's capacity for intellectualization. Indeed, there were special reasons why the elementary school child was the perfect subject for this approach. First of all, given his level of maturation,[17] the intellectual manipulations required in the traditional method could not be expected of him. Second, his limitations in reading and writing English excluded the possibility of exposing him to those skills in the foreign language if one wished to avoid the risk of confusion and "contamination." By elimination, the FLES student was a perfect candidate for a purely audio-lingual approach.

But besides the logic inherent in the above, more positive arguments were adduced. If, indeed, the new method involved automatic control achieved through repeated exposure to a model mastered through massive repetition, it followed that the young child (the younger the better) was the most likely subject to succeed. It became public knowledge that, in the early years, a part of the cortex remained "uncommitted," an area ready to absorb additional language input without competition or interference from the native language.[18] Third, it was generally agreed that the young child was least resistant to the fatigue resulting from repetition, least demanding to know why language was the way it was or why he was being exposed to it in the first place. Last, because of their general lack of inhibition, youngsters were most receptive to "acting out," the role-playing involved in dialogue presentation.

Public demand and the documentation provided by the profession constituted strong pressure on administrations to initiate programs. The more reluctant, those wary of major investments in developing foreign-language skills, rationalized their capitulation on the basis that the implications for developing multicultural sensitivities through the foreign-language class was a goal consistent with preparing the new generation for full political and social roles in the best interest of a newly emerging cosmopolitan world.

In brief, money was found to support instruction, schedules were modified to accommodate the foreign-language class, the necessary audiovisual aids were usually provided, and FLES enrollment doubled from 1959 to 1965.[19]

There have been a number of reasons advanced for the decline in momentum of the FLES movement. That many programs were initiated without considered judgement, adequate preparation, or qualified staff simply to be competitive in the academic status race is undeniable.[20] That many programs were handicapped because, since qualified experienced teachers were not available, these programs had to resort to makeshift staffing arrangements doomed to be unproductive, is also a matter of record.[21]

But to blame the regression on these factors alone or on the overall recession of available funds seems a facile way of avoiding recognition of more fundamental and complex factors.

The conditions under which FLES was spectacularly launched contained in great part the elements of its eventual decline. For, the same enthusiasm that made its inception possible was infused into predictions of miraculous results. Given the combination of positive factors listed previously, FLES was to demonstrate the feasibility of acquiring a high level of fluency in a foreign language relatively quickly and, more important, less painfully than with other methods.

"Bilingualism" became loosely associated with the product of FLES instruction. Though undefined by those optimistically using the term and insufficiently questioned by those in the profession who knew better, it symbolized categorical expectations easily assimilated by the public. And though expectancies are instrumental in multiplying momentum, they also serve as a devastating criterion if and when such expectancies are not met. By the time it became evident that the predictions for "bilingual" command had not materialized,[22] by the time the profession retrenched on the more modest claim that FLES was essential and productive as part of the "long sequence" that foreign-language study necessitates, the fate of FLES had already been foretold.[23]

Paradoxically, the inseparability of the FLES concept from the purest expression of the audiolingual philosophy did not, in the long run, serve it well. Although, by and large, the appropriateness of the method as a dominant mode of instruction is unquestionable, a number of doctrinaire caveats considered by many as integral to the method complicated instruction in many settings.

Complete avoidance of English in the foreign-language class limited the possibility of developing teacher-student rapport, of explanations of purpose, of establishing harmonious procedures, all of which are of paramount importance to children in the lower grades.

The taboo of "translation" resulted in many students emerging from several years of instruction with some fluency on a well-drilled corpus of material but, unfortunately, no notion what they were saying, where it might be said, or in what ways the elements memorized could be recombined into meaningful communication.

The recommendation of indefinite deferment of exposure to the printed word did not serve well the visually oriented students who had already demonstrated limited aural discrimination. Furthermore, after a year or two of exposure, the average student, who normally associates learning with books and written exercises, often tended to demean the language class as limiting and frivolous. For the most gifted students, especially in upper grades, total avoidance of "rules" and explanations that smacked of the old grammar approach left him frustrated; contrary to his other subjects, the foreign-language class proscribed the use of his recognized intellectual potential.

In a more general and more significant sense, the elementary setting was seen as a proving ground for the audio-lingual method rather than as a testing ground where FLES practices would be studied, tested, and modified as a means of assuring continuous development of an emerging program.[24] Assessment was directed primarily at the orthodoxy of the teacher's use of the method rather than on the reaction of the class.[25] Such research as was mounted addressed itself to the effectiveness of the method in terms of achievement rather than on the more basic problems of motivation, learning rate, and so on, which might have been studied more productively with the unsophisticated youngsters than at any subsequent stage.[26]

Another paradox resides in the fact that FLES, in order to be consistent with the democratic concept of American education, tended to be open to all students. This automatically involved a wide range of aptitudes and attitudes calling for a flexible teaching strategy and setting forth a variety of objectives. In other words, teachers were suddenly faced with all the problems attending instruction of heterogeneous groups. We are not sure that even the best foreign-language teachers, wrestling with new curricula, often dealing with an age level with which they were not familiar could pay proper attention to this formidable challenge, especially since their own previous experience typically involved gifted, well-motivated, and more mature students.

The irony is that enthusiasm for FLES is declining at a time when, as a result of experience, the movement is indeed better prepared to deal more realistically and effectively with the student population.[27]

The teacher is presently less constrained by the fetishism of "pure" methodology.[28] Earlier initiation to reading skills is viewed with greater tolerance[29] and the exploitation of the young student's intellegence in addition to his capacity for mim-mem is currently admitted to be an asset rather than a liability.

There are also indications that serious consideration is being given to measuring the effect (based on student responsiveness) of early exposure to foreign language in developing positive attitudes toward the subject at both the linguistic and cultural levels as an area at least as important as measurement of the language skills.[30] In the latter area more realistic goals have been set, goals that measure the relative extent of preparation rather than absolute standards relating to "bilingual" command.

Dealing with heterogeneous groups has suggested assessment of achievement on a relative basis and opened the way to elaborating materials and teaching strategies consistent with the canons of individualized instruction.

Teachers, though still too few, have demonstrated their capacity for growth, their flexibility, and their continuing development of expertise. The spirit of innovation resulting in the production of impressive TV programs and a wide assortment of audiovisual aids is still characteristic of the FLES teachers, who can now fall back on an exhaustive literature dealing with materials, methodology, and evaluation.

But FLES is still being undermined by the lack of serious support from the foreign-language teachers at other levels. Lack of communication and consensus resulting in the much-publicized problem of articulation still continues to be punitive to the elementary school child entering high school and deleterious to the maintenance of FLES programs.[31]

Implications

The preceding brief overview of FLES serves to outline a number of strands characteristic of the foreign-language scene prior to 1970. These basic trends will be summarized and discussed in more detail as a means of establishing the current position of foreign-language teaching.

The FLES movement reflects popular acceptance of foreign-language instruction as a viable subject in the curriculum. It illustrates the trend of the last generation to expose all students to a foreign language at as early an age as possible and for a long enough period to ensure command of that language, particularly with reference to the conversational skills. Increased foreign-language enrollment at the secondary level with consequent increase at the college level is consistent with this trend.

Inversely, the decline of FLES in the 60s is also paralleled by a decline in overall enrollment. Using 100 as an index in 1960, we find total enrollment rising to 180 in 1967 and stabilizing over the next three years. Though the figures do not reflect an actual decline in the total number of students enrolled, they are interpreted as worrisome in that they do not show an increase proportionate to an increasing school population and a greater percentage of that population continuing their education, particularly at the college level.[32]

Increased enrollment inevitably resulted in a teacher shortage with consequent support for teacher-training programs. Less tangible but perhaps as important, the foreign-language profession was infused with a spirit of optimism and self-assurance that resulted in greater self-identity, commitment to professional goals, and systematic development of effective professional activities.

Instructing a greater number of pupils also raised a number of problems for the teacher, who, at the elementary and secondary level in particular, had to deal with a more heterogeneous population and thus modify his concept of the school as a "screening" agency to that of the class as providing several kinds of productive experiences at different levels depending on the aptitudes of the pupils. It follows that this change in philosophical posture resulted in greater flexibility in setting goals and devising appropriate instructional strategies for meeting these goals. Inevitably the teacher is being pushed in the direction of individualized instruction.

The acceptance of FLES in already crowded elementary curriculum is of fundamental importance. Along with parallel emphasis on foreign languages in the secondary schools, it represents a major (though temporary) shift in the conception of the curriculum. Acceptance of the notion that command of a foreign language and exposure to its culture contributes to the life-style of the young American citizen, as we have seen, was related to the national concern for defense and the establishment of a new American image in a shrinking world dreaming of eternal peace through international understanding. Related to this posture was the thrust of educational "revisionists" such as Conant and others, who (temporarily, at least) preached a doctrine of no-nonsense education, a basic return to emphasis on subject-matter instruction as the primary function of the schools.

The audio-lingual approach was also legitimized by the fact that it was consonant with new curricular trends. As in mathematics and sciences, for instance, new materials designed for national impact were the products of cooperative efforts involving theorists, practitioners, and media specialists. In the case of foreign languages we find that, in the best "new" tradition, all of these conditions were fulfilled. Linguists provided the theoretical framework. Psychologists, especially those strongly slanted toward a Skinnerian doctrine, saw the mim-mem practice, in class or in the lab, as completely justified. Avant-garde teachers at·the college and high-school level were eager to cooperate at the implementation and evaluation phase of pilot programs. Last, the repetition inherent in the method combined with the stimulus-response-reward doctrine to justify extensive investments in tape recorders, laboratories, and so forth, as necessary mechanical adjuncts. The movie clip was self-evidently a superb medium for exposing students to "authentic" scenes of the culture in question. Teacher shortage suggested television as an alternate mode of instruction. In short, mass instruction in foreign languages conformed to all the canons of the period as pronounced by psychology, linguistics, technology. These, in turn, were translated into practices by the joint effort of theorists and practitioners.

3   Assessment

Let us now consider in greater detail the evaluation of these
several areas over a period of some ten years, particularly as
they relate to implementation and evaluation, the relationship of
theory to practice, of promise to achievement. In each case, I shall
again limit the material to significant highlights and refer the
reader to the appropriate literature for amplification and further
documentation.

Linguistics

Though the impact of linguistics on foreign-language teaching
has been enormous, it must be made clear at the outset that
linguists were responsible only for the exposition of a number of
linguistic principles and claimed no expertise in translating these
principles into effective classroom practices. As a matter of fact,
they are on record as advisedly rejecting all responsibility for
pedagogical concerns as early as 1952. Fries states unequivocally:

> As a scientist the linguist is searching for pure knowledge. To
> know the facts and to understand the language processes are to
> him ends in themselves. He usually leaves to others the business of
> applying practically the knowledge he has won.[1]

To the chagrin of many foreign-language specialists, this position
was reiterated by Chonsky in the course of the 1966 Northeast
Conference.

And yet, for many years, foreign-language teachers felt a
direct or indirect pressure to be knowledgeable about linguistics
as the fountainhead prerequisite to implementation of the "New
Key." To this end a number of works such as Ferguson's
Linguistic Reading Lists for Teachers of Modern Languages
(1963)[2] and Halliday and others' *The Linguistic Sciences and*

Language Teaching (1964)[3] provided the profession with handy road maps for the field. Such incursions, however, often served merely as a frustrating experience to the majority of practitioners. The level of abstraction of the content, the obfuscating nomenclature, the proliferation of subdisciplines (psycholinguistics, biolinguistics, sociolinguistics, etc.) contributed to a sense of futility in the best-trained teacher even when he had time and energy to devote to a systematic pursuit of the subject.

Fortunately, applied linguists constituted themselves as intermediaries between theory and practice. Belasco's *Anthology*,[4] several subsequent major series[5] dealing primarily with phonemics and structure, a number of significant books,[6] and countless articles in professional journals served to translate linguistic principles into operational terms for the teacher.[7]

In spite of the legitimacy of linguistic tenets, they were harmonized into "New Key" methodology with sometimes capricious, sometimes peculiar effects, which can be attributed at least in part to blind faith and consequent zeal.

Commitment to the primacy of speech does suggest fluent production approximating, as nearly as possible, an authentic native model. As a terminal goal it implies mastering to a point of automaticity the surface structures inherent in the message. Achievement of this goal presupposes practice in the foreign language rather than explication of its grammatical features. But, since practice involves massive doses of repetitive exercises, rigid adherence to this position raises problems in a class situation. During the intermediary phases leading to terminal achievement, students tend to become bored by the process and discouraged as they consider the road yet to be covered.

Forcing the student to "think" in the foreign language is a sound principle but one that, unfortunately, is not always practical in dealing with classroom management or developing the kind of interpersonal communication necessary in "humanizing" the foreign-language experience. Complete avoidance of English also precludes blending a judicious dose of sophisticated cultural concepts into the early phases of skill development. At a more functional level there is evidence that the tour de force of staying in the second language (as practiced by a few exceptionally gifted practitioners) is often beyond the capabilities of the majority of teachers. It is generally agreed that visuals substituted for English verbal cues are not guaranteed to suggest the same referent to all viewers, that some concepts are extremely difficult to pantomine, that, even when successful, the process of visual association is extremely time-consuming in contrast to the process of using English cues. We are basically in accord with Fernand Marty's position:

> Whenever possible, the sentence where the new word appears for the first time should reveal its meaning; if this is not possible the teacher sould try to explain the meaning of the new word either with a *rapid* explanation, a *rapid* drawing, or a *rapid* mimic; if this takes too long (more than ten seconds) it is preferable to give the English equivalent. Let us remember that our goal is to teach the language in the shortest possible time; we are not trying to perform the *tour de force* of teaching French without using a single word of English.[8]

Furthermore, it is sometimes argued that students cannot be prevented from referring to English equivalents, especially under academic stress. In my own experience, students faced with making free response to a picture will respond to the extent of their memorized repertoire. Faced with an unknown referent in the picture, their reaction is predictably "What's the word for ————?" The following example suggests that total avoidance of English equivalents can result in misinterpretation for some students and total mystification for others:

> It happened in Thailand, according to Peggy Swallows, a Peace Corps volunteer teaching English in that country.
> Teacher: This is a chair.
> Chorus of students: This is a chair.
> Teacher: Mango.
> Students: This is a mango.
> Teacher: Table.
> Students: This is a table.
> Teacher: That.
> Students: This is a that.

Teacher: No, think please!
Student A: This is a think please.
Teacher: No, a thousand times no! (Pause)
Very bright student: This is a table.
Teacher: ah! Correct . . . . Eye.
Student B: I is a table.
(Exit teacher)[9]

It would be difficult to argue against memorization of dialogues as an effective way of promoting native production in terms of pronunciation, spontaneity, unconscious command of structures, in short, as a total language experience including latent cultural implications.

To achieve this kind of command implies modeling and producing speech at a speed normal for the native. The resulting exchange, regardless of lexical and structural content, would indeed be authentic. In practice, many problems are raised. In some cases, the less-gifted student finds himself unable to register the total utterance, let alone reproduce it. Even for those capable of memorizing and reproducing the total utterance in this style, there remains the problem of delineating word boundaries, identifying components of the utterances that, eventually, must become entities in a linguistic repertoire available for re-combination whether they be manupulative or "automatic."
We tend to forget that the principle of normal speed of delivery is not consistently adhered to even for native speakers in the early years of language training. Teachers in the lower grades tend to overenunciate (a characteristic that is often manifest outside the classroom). We think also of Topaze's special style for dictées in Pagnol's play.

The "authentic model" also raises problems in terms of incremental content of the dialogue. The structures are randomly included as needed to reproduce a "normal" conversation. During initial exposure to the dialogue, each of these must be attacked as separate vocabulary items. Since they are many and since only a few can be treated in any one unit in the structural drill that follows, the majority remain a problem for massive rote-learning, unsupported by any organizing principle.

It is difficult to reconcile in retrospect how the dialogue

progressed from being useful to being indispensable. And yet, many basic texts from beginning to end base each unit on an initial dialogue, insensitive to the proposition that any experience, no matter how productive, eventually becomes tedious. It must be noted that students gave methodologists ample opportunity to reconsider and adjust. Past a given point, entire classes refused to memorize the dialogue. It is curious that, with the emphasis put on the dialogue as central to the method, so little research was conducted to determine what might have made memorization easier (length of each line, total number of lines, etc.) or when "saturation" normally occurred.

The principle of "automaticity," again a valid linguistic goal, is also associated, in the mind of many (students and teachers), with exaggerated insistence on relentless practice. This condition was acerbated by the fact that, in many instances, insufficient explanations by the teacher forced the students to go through endless exercises unaware of why they were doing them or of what purpose their docile efforts served. The emerging "generalization," for many, came too late. Others would have done better if they had started with the "generalization" as a peg on which to hang (and justify) the whole procedure.

Perhaps inadvertantly, the linguist's concern with structures served to relegate "vocabulary" to a kind of pedagogical limbo. It has already been noted that establishing verbal equivalence between two terms was considered a deleterious practice. Furthermore, the new credo proscribed the learning of words "out of context." It was, furthermore, the plea that "vocabulary" deserved this demotion since the Mad Hatter had proved that one knew quite a bit about a certain communication even when the utterance gave no clue to any specific referent.[10]

It is possible that this was simply overacting against the "traditional" vocabulary list, which was allegedly responsible for many of the woes of language learners in a less enlightened epoch. For many, groups of words within a context were never identified as lexical entities, stems never differentiated from prefixes or suffixes, and function words never recognized as central to the content of the utterance. It seemed to make no difference whether

the "boy bit the dog" or the "dog bit the boy" provided it was
clearly understood that somebody was doing something to
someone else. This in spite of that fact that at least a portion of
the student population using visual or verbal stimuli would have
learned well the words "boy," "bit," and "dog," would have
enjoyed manipulating the three items to form different utterances
and, having played with the alternatives, would have been
impressed with the possibility of utilizing vocabulary and
structure to "create" concepts that could be tested against
"reality," or at least plausibility.

Contrastive linguistics saw as one of its important contributions the identification and categorizing of "area of interference," principally those inherent in the phonology and
structure of English as opposed to a foreign language. This served
to predict what language difficulties would be most stubborn to
overcome and consequently what concentration of effort would be
most appropriate to eradicate native habits. But again, some
interpreted this constructive endeavor, which is indeed an
important part of language learning, as a subsititute for other
efforts related to the total task. In the same way that it was
assumed that vocabulary is no problem provided that structures
are internalized, by overconcentration on contrastive features a
number of "systems" take for granted that parallel structures will
be assimilated. The result is constant wrestling with the most
difficult aspect of language without "cashing in" on the easier
(more immediately rewarding) factors. This sometimes results in
mastery of an isolated problem with no accretion of skill in those
areas where a modicum of attention would have given better
perception of the total context.

The idea of "contrast" even permeated the cultural dimension. In the area of "pure" culture, it resulted in insistence
on the idiosyncratic rather than on a broad spectrum of
commonly shared values and customs. This perception related
obliquely to the presentation of "vocabulary in context." Dispro-
portionate importance was placed on the cultural differences
implicit in the use of *tu* and *vous*, on the connotation of *vin* for
different cultures, without a balancing statement that for a great

number of referents in a variety of utterances no conceptual contrast exists between English and Western European countries, at least in modern times.

As has been noted, commitment to the primacy of speech resulted in linguists' concentrating on the conversational skills. This productive exercise of their expertise in the area of aural comprehension and speaking hardly explains the organized campaign against reading and writing that marked the early years of the audio-lingual period. The consequences have been serious. First of all, interest was shifted from "reading," the skill in which the profession, through the works of West, Bond, and others, had made substantial systematic progress. Second, it tended to move foreign languages out of the sphere of other "solid" subjects reliant on "the book" as a primary medium of instruction. (It must be said that these other subjects also saw themselves moving toward more "progressive" media in the early 50s.) It also doomed the visually oriented and aurally limited student to failure. Last, because reading and writing were tabooed as a goal, they were unavailable as a means of improving the aural-oral skills.

The consequence has been a sterile period during which the relationship of the oral skills to reading and writing has been neglected. The problems raised by reexamination of the strictly audio-lingual position suggests that, in the next decade, contrastive linguists might well turn their attention to problems attending interferences that occur in the transition from hearing-speaking to reading-writing or, inversely, to a new, more flexible concept of sequencing uninhibited by notions of what is the "proper" sequence.

An inordinate amount of time has been devoted to arguments concerning what sequence is best in exposure to the various skills. The long, inconclusive, erudite, and informative debate has argued as if each of the skills had primacy as an end in itself. Thus, if speaking were the goal, the practice of speaking was seen as the sole way of reaching the goal. Inversely, in reading courses, time devoted to the spoken language was minimized as stealing time from the sole, predetermined end.

This kind of polarity has tended to obscure the consideration of any individual skill as a means. And yet we have some experience that contrasting the written forms of *le*, *la*, *les*, with simultaneous, correct modeling of each, may be an effective way, through a visual cue, of overcoming the English speaker's tendency to level nondiscriminatory prefixation. For a certain student, to copy a word a certain number of times may be the most appropriate way of learning spelling while at the same time adding that word to his active vocabulary. Likewise, reading individual words or passages may facilitate memorization of either the words or the complete passage, or at least facilitate comprehension of the same recorded message, a process superior to repetition, which often leads to frustration rather than to progressive improvement in comprehension.

It is true that understanding and speaking require "instantaneous" decoding and coding, respectively. But some serious attention to the process of developing these skills to a fine point must be given serious thought. Utilization of the written word passively and actively, because it provides a static record, may be instrumental in developing that process.

Psychology

If Skinner had not been "professing" around 1955, foreign-language theorists would have invented him. In retrospect, it is difficult to imagine how the profession, while seeming to ignore deliberately other "schools" of psychology, chose to ground its practices solely in Skinnerian precepts. A partial explanation lies in the fact that in the original phase of audio-lingualism the hopes and aspirations of foreign-language methodologists had been focused on a narrow but promising objective: to achieve language control by developing a set of habits to the point of automaticity.

Skinner's position reinforced the militant audio-lingualist's vision of panacea supported by psychological research. At the same time, it served to justify the rejection of practices associated with the horrendous failure of the "traditional" approach, those cognitive activities (learning about the language, manipulating vocabulary in terms of grammatical rules, etc.) that were allegedly deleterious to the learner and had proved fatal to the cause of foreign-language instruction.

Given the impact of such documents as Skinner's "The Science of Learning and the Art of Teaching,"[11] I do not intend to minimize the important contribution that the Law of Effect can make to particular tasks in particular language-learning situations. Nor do I quarrel with the value of positive rewards in contrast to evasive rewards, to the efficacy of immediate reinforcement, to the importance of the scheduled frequency of these reinforcements. Nor do I disagree with Skinner's views that the teacher is normally incapable of arranging the necessary contingencies effectively and sufficiently for each student and that this speaks to greater sequential control through programs and mechanical devices (the laboratory, for instance). I am suggesting that the Skinnerian doctrine as it applies to foreign-language learning provides an essential direction, a valid part to be judiciously integrated into the complex totality of the learning task.[12]

But even this simplistic reduction as applied to the artificial conditions attending second-language learning was not long in creating discomfort among both theorists and practioners. As early as 1963 Lambert elaborated on the complexity of foreign-language learning as an academic activity, particularly in view of the external motivational factor that Skinner minimizes in his approach.[13] In 1964 Ausubel raised the question of a single approach as appropriate to all age levels, maintaining that "certain features of the audio-lingual approach are psychologically incompatible with effective learning processes in adults."[14] Eventually, many came to agree that even under the "controlled" conditions best achieved in the language laboratory the students did not respond as predictably as Skinner's pigeons. The fact that each in his own way was more individualistic and more complex than the experimental birds is probably responsible in part for raising such questions as when a "reward" ceases to be a reward, that is, when does boredom born of repetition obliterate the effect of short-termed reward? For foreign-language studies in particular, when does the difficulty of the task, the prospect of unending continuation without a powerful, long-range, tangible reward related to a basic need affect the effectiveness of the process? Or how does the experience itself tend to be rejected insofar as it lacks a "human dimension," does not exploit other "tools" available to students, and goes contrary to inquiry-oriented practices prevailing in the context of what students have been led to believe constitutes meaningful education?

Indeed, during the last ten years, while a number of language theorists have maintained the position that a Skinnerian approach did produce the expected results, a growing volume of literature aimed either at refuting the narrow view implied in pure audio-lingualism or motivated by concerns independent of second-language teaching and learning problems has tended to highlight the complexities inherent in the teaching-learning combination as it applied to education in general and to second-language learning in particular.[15]

As an indication of how far the pendulum has swung away from faith to heretical doubt, the following quotation describes the path traveled in little more than a decade:

When they gather at regional and national meetings, foreign language teachers are no longer invited to share in the excitement of new methodological directions. Instead, they are warned of the limitations of various aspects of the audio-lingual approach—if they are not apprised of the complete lack of substance in its theoretical underpinnings.[16]

The positions of Ausubel, Gagné, and Bruner, insofar as they contradict in various degrees the noncognitive Skinnerian approach, cannot be overlooked if we are to consider foreign-language learning as more than purely mechanistic activity. Furthermore, since these psychologists have had a deep influence on curriculum in general, it is important to note their respective theses as applicable to foreign-language instruction and to note how exclusion of their influence has tended to make foreign-language study vulnerable from the curricular perspective.

For Ausubel, learning (including memorization of disparate language items) is facilitated if learning is meaningful, that is, if students can relate new materials to a structure already existing at the cognitive level. In the case of foreign-language study where, initially, the student has no preconceived cognitive structure, the teacher is responsible for providing the "organizers," ranging from those having wide explanatory power, generalizability, and reliability to more discrete ones focusing on a specific set of linguistic phenomena (grammar rules, in some instances), which provide a cognitive framework for the student and determine the organization and arrangement of class activities including practice drills and feedback.[17]

Gagné emphasized the sequential nature of efficient learning and sees the student moving through a series of increasingly complicated processes each of which assumes successful completion at the prior level, which is reinforced in the learner's mind by his capability to move to the new task.[18] In Gagné's system, the teacher's responsibility is to set up a sequence in such a way that optimum mediation will occur as the student progresses through successive levels of complexity. This implies a clear conceptualization of the ultimate task and the appropriateness of the contributing components toward continuous movement in the direction of the final task.

Bruner is more concerned with the process of learning than with a particular goal toward which learning activities are directed. While discovery learning develops the student's capacity for information gathering and for organizing that information, it not only leads to his internalization of the material but the principal reward in the act of discovery itself, which is a stimulus for repeating the process sequentially directed at problems of increasing complexity.[19] The teacher is flexible in setting goals congenial to the student's interests. He becomes a source of the "information" and cues that will best serve the child in solving the problem. In the last analysis, the teacher is committed to accept the solution emerging from the student's involvement in his own style of inquiry. This does not necessarily mean that "wrong" solutions are accepted but rather that their discrepancy with "facts" serves as the stimulus for more refined and sophisticated modes of inquiry.

The inappropriateness (one may even say the danger) of the discovery method is obvious if one considers solely the accretion of language skills: for a child to "discover" the correct spelling or pronunciation of a word or utterance is counterproductive if his conclusions do not coincide with the linguistic "facts" of the case. And yet this does not preclude the use of a Brunerian approach if one wishes to develop sensitivity to language phenomena (semantics, for instance) or to approach the study of culture through open-ended discussion.

The nature of the student-teacher relationship is obviously modified by the psychological stance adopted. For Ausubel and Gagné the teacher plays a superordinate role in determining the structure and content of the learning activity. For Bruner the teacher is the mediator, and the child, engaged in discovery, takes on the superordinate role. The problem of "effectiveness," ever a teacher's concern, is also viewed differently. Ausubel sees "discovery" as time-consuming, particularly for adults already capable of grasping the conceptualization of others, while Bruner, by focusing on the process of inquiry, has little concern for the fact that the product may be inconsistent with the acceptable "truth" of the conclusion (e.g., the problem of "discovering" a new spelling for a word).

Whether one sees the functioning of "organizers" as facilitating the learning task when preceding that task, as espoused by Ausubel, or wishes to espouse the sequential, capability-producing, programmatic approach characteristic of Gagné or explore the possibility of process development through Bruner's discovery method, the question is not so much the validity of each of these positions or their merits relative to each other but rather which one is applicable to a particular situation for a given student attempting to complete a given task. It is easy to project a situation in which, in connection with any language phenomenon, the simultaneous use of several approaches will serve to identify the one approach that is more congenial to a given population and/or the extent to which all approaches reinforce each other with resultant improvement in learning.

For instance, the student may be required to repeat (with appropriate rewards) until he reaches the point of automatic response (Skinner):

> je chantais
> tu chantais
> il chantait

The task might be facilitated if as a preface to the repetition drill it is pointed out that in this exercise there is not phonetic difference in suffixation and that attention should be focused on the initial prefix as the significant discriminator (Ausubel).

In addition, the situation can be programmed so that (given the principle of similar endings) the student on the basis of the single model *je chantais* develops the capacity to respond correctly to the stimulus *tu* and *il* (Gagné).

Last, once the paradigm has been mastered orally, it can be submitted to the student in writing. He will be led to "discover" that there is a final consonant for each utterance, that it is silent in all cases, that the ending is "s" in the first two instances but shifts to "t" in the case of the third person. He may be further encouraged to "discover" the generalizability of the situation or come to some further generalization that (in this case at least) morphological discrimination is made possible through prefixation rather than suffixation (Bruner).

Generally, and in spite of the defensiveness of exponents of the pure audio-lingual method, a semblance of rationality has been interjected into the picture, a tendency to identify problems rather than ignore them, to deal with complexity on a selective basis rather than to rely on broad approximations.

The many ways in which native-language learning differs from the second-language learning in an artificial situation have been stressed with resultant clarification of the confusion inherent in equating the two processes. We are less prone to disregard these differences in terms of saturation time, intrinsic motivation, and the development of language skills "scheduled" by gradual development of psychomotor and cognitive skills. Conversely, fewer are inclined to treat the second language learner as if he did not bring to task an already sophisticated linguistic apparatus.

"Coordinate" bilingualism, the ability to "think" in the language one is speaking as do persons brought up in regions where two or more languages are in current use, is more rarely considered feasible as a result of a few years of exposure in school. Many teachers will now settle realistically for such proficiency in the second language as has been achieved by a respectable number of "compound" bilinguals, who, initially at least, relied heavily on their native language to formulate expressions in the foreign tongue.

It has been pointed out that the kind of linguistic performance demonstrated by facile repetition of pattern drills and other exercises does not necessarily equate ability to communicate meaningfully in the foreign language and that more than rote-learning is involved in developing competence in the deeper linguistic processes necessary to genuine communication.

The relationship of skill development to motivational factors is being reconsidered. Neither the instrumental learner concerned primarily with learning a language for the specific purpose of obtaining a job abroad or of passing a reading exam nor the integrative learner seeing in foreign-language study the opportunity to satisfy his curiosity and compulsion can be expected to react positively to a course that is too general in its objectives or to one that, because it is too narrow, prescribes activities unrelated to the learner's objectives.

The issue of transfer has been raised again as of central interest. It is being viewed more broadly than simply transferring the application of learning habits or overcoming difficulties emerging from interferences existing between one language and another.

Further distinctions will hopefully facilitate transfer from one language skill to another and from a basic attitude toward a language to the cultural matrix of that language (and vice versa). Transfer is being seen not only as depending on the degree to which two languages are alike or dissimilar but also as influenced by the teacher's understanding of the task to be performed and the learner's perception of what he is to do.

In short, increasingly attention is being turned to individualizing skill objectives to make the task expected more palatable to students of various predilections and learning styles. Finally, more consideration is being given to the student's perception of the process in which he is supposedly actively engaged: his interpretation of long-range objectives, of the efficacy of long-range objectives, of the efficacy of immediate rewards, of the relevance of the task to his expectations, and of the measure in which self-expectations and self-diagnosis will contribute to his remaining actively engaged.[20]

Although facing up to increasing complexity at the theoretical and research level is indeed salutary and eventually promises recommendations for improved instructional stratagems, these endeavors provide few immediate resources to the practitioner. He has probably learned to shy away from total commitment to any single position since each represents only a specialized point of view on a continuum. It is hardly logical to expect the practitioner to make the synthesis that the respective psychologists feel beyond their purview.[21]

In the meantime, while attempting to be knowledgeable about new theories and the results of current research, the teacher must content himself with general guidelines representative of the consensus of various schools. Checking himself out against these generalities might be a useful step pending the emergence of reliable theories that can be tested for their applicability in the classroom.[22]

Technology

Electronic devices are often considered essential to the implementation of the audio-lingual method. Historical precedents for consistent use of mechanical aids go back to the army programs. The wire recorder, commercially available shortly after World War II and eventually converted into the tape recorder as we know it, spared the teacher much of the fatigue attending "rote-teaching" drills. At the same time, the sound track controlled the speed of delivery and provided a variety of authentic models of pronunciation and intonation.

The picture of the itinerant teacher toting his trusted tape recorder on his appointed rounds is still familiar. In many settings it was replaced by the more impressive battery of apparatus constituting the language laboratory. The advantages of linking a number of ear sets and microphones through a central console are many. At a minimal level students can multiply their rate of participation by individually responding to each stimulus provided by a single program emanating from the console. In many instances, the console can emit a number of programs simultaneously, thus providing the student the opportunity to select the program most appropriate to his need. Better systems permit the students to listen directly to his responses as he checks them against a given program. The more sophisticated installations provide for recording facilities at each position. The student, having once recorded the master program on one track, can record his own responses on the other track and subsequently replay alternatively the model and his own rendition in order to compare, analyze, and eventually duplicate the original model.[23]

From the console the teacher usually has facilities for monitoring and counseling individual students. In addition to multiplying participation, individualizing selections, and providing opportunity for self-evaluation, the laboratory system also provides an atmosphere of privacy particularly protective to those students sensitive to having their progress (or lack thereof) exposed to the entire class. Used as a library facility, the laboratory provides opportunity for further individualized instruction.

In some cases the audio track is (in or out of the laboratory) synchronized with visual stimuli intended to elicit responses or to provide association between referents and verbal equivalents. Filmstrips and slides often are essential features of the audio-visual packages.[24]

Films are also used extensively in developing linguistic skills. Films can provide an authentic set for language activities and, in addition to the purely language-teaching function, are the medium par excellence for authentic presentation of a foreign culture.[25]

Extensive programs were structured in the hope that TV presentations would compensate in part for the limitations (in number and in quality) of the available teaching force. The Midwest Program on Airborne Television Instruction[26] and particularly *Parlons Français*[27] represent two different approaches to scheduling teacher preparation and classroom follow-up. Both efforts represent a sophisticated effort to utilize educational television in foreign-language teaching.[28]

A number of programs intended to facilitate individualized instruction appeared on the market in the early 1960s. Others are being developed, but there is little evidence that, to date, programmed instruction has had serious impact on the profession.[29]

Lastly, although foreign-language specialists are conscious of the potential of computerized instruction, work in this area is still in a preliminary developmental stage and an effective product is still a long way from being available for general classroom use.[30]

The rise and fall in the popularity of the language laboratory is a phenomenon that perhaps best illustrates some of the problems besetting effective utilization of technology. Even though there is less apprehension (openly expressed, at least) on the part of teachers that they will be replaced by the mechanical unit, certain arguments still militate against use of any medium as more than incidental to the basic course.

1. Cost. Both the initial investment in hardware and the need to constantly supply the machine with appropriate software cannot be justified unless this cost is amortized through constant and effective use. In this respect, manufacturers have been their own worst enemies. The high cost of initial product that obviously includes developmental expenditures is seldom cut back as volume sale is achieved.

2. Maintenance. Even the simple tape recorder or filmstrip viewer needs periodic service by someone better qualified than the average teacher. The malfunction of any piece of equipment, particularly when it is as complex as a laboratory installation,

is disastrous in the view of the teacher on whom responsibility for controlling the class is made difficult by the breakdown of the planned activity.

3. Software. The teacher is usually in a dilemma in this respect. Either the software is the program and gives the teacher a feeling of futility in terms of personal objectives and teaching style, or the software is incidental to the "course," in which case the teacher is frustrated by the difficult need to select, purchase, and articulate the software with the "book" or syllabus. Additionally, many audiovisual aids are of poor quality. In some cases, it is hard to decide where and when and for what purpose they might best be made a part of a coherent program.

4. Impersonality. Audio and visual aids as processed through mechanical devices tend to reduce the amount of personal interaction that, in the eyes of many teachers, is particularly essential to language learning and the process of communication.

The above, with such other considerations as scheduling difficulty, rigidity of operation, and lack of student response, have led to a decreased emphasis on technology as instrumental to improved instruction. This may in part have been acerbated by insistence on teaching the skills of speaking and understanding through media without a sufficiently detailed breakdown as to where and in what way technology would most efficiently serve the teacher at the subskill level.

Culture

Sometimes listed as a fifth objective for language learners, the area of culture has certainly stimulated more than one fifth of the attention of the foreign-language profession in the last fifteen years. For, if an important justification for foreign-language study consists in improving international relations, it follows that mastering language skills is but a prerequisite to achieving the goal: language itself must be used "correctly" in the total cultural context and, furthermore, supralinguistic aspects of communication must be enhanced through the student's knowing about, functioning in, and being duly open-minded to the societal dimensions of the culture whose language is being studied.

In considering a broader definition of culture the profession did not overtly condemn the traditional concept of culture as reflected in the artistic production of a nation as the highest summation of a people's cultural heritage. It would have been foolhardy to denigrate literature, painting, music, and other art forms as inconsequential to the national heritage. But because art forms were considered the ultimate level of cultural activities, productive exposure to literature as an important cultural domain presupposed a maximum of linguistic preparation. Theoretically, this type of study cannot be integrated into the language sequence until the more advanced stages. In practice, however, many teachers feel compelled to expose students prematurely to literary study, with disastrous effect. Teachers often insist on hacking their way through the "classics," though these texts are usually beyond the linguistic capacities of the class. This usually results in painful sessions during which a negative attitude toward literature develops and, by extension, a dour view of all facets of foreign-language instruction.

The new emphasis shifted to those aspects of culture that permeated the daily lives of the people, which were fundamental to the societal fabric that, by providing a total context, would facilitate "understanding" of what to an American might be considered idiosyncratic behavior. Culture became defined increasingly in terms of anthropology and sociology with a view to identifying and codifying significant patterns rather than in terms of the work of art, which, of necessity, is individualistically conceived and sociologically selective.

The task of definition, selection, and application to the language class has proved both enormous and frustrating as the voluminous literature of the past decades will attest.

Obviously, turning to the Human Relations Area Files, though a legitimate first move, proved relatively unproductive.[31] The merits of each file was, at the same time, its most serious limitation: though providing a good checklist, it was simply too encompassing to permit transformation into functional classroom units. And over the years the work of Brooks,[32] Nostrand,[33] and Seelye,[34] among others,[35] constitutes a rich documentation of an effort to define by restriction and to simplify for the purpose of providing an operational base.

It may be that, as a heuristic device at least, the topic of culture may be considered as three overlapping categories. The first includes the way in which cultural factors are inseparable from communication, that is, how language reflects connotations peculiar to a culture, how various social conditions affect choice of vocabulary and structures, how gestures and accompanying physical behavior are socially as well as linguistically determined.[36] A second (and still very broad area) is constituted by variances in the ways people of different cultures conceive interpersonal relationships, and the predetermined role an individual must play as he is influenced by beliefs, traditions, social and political institutions, economic conditions, and other normative influences. The third category is concerned with the affect that knowing about the first two has upon an individual outside the foreign culture. As he increases his knowledge is he more understanding, more accepting? Has he internalized cultural features to the point that he can function in a foreign context?

In spite of the vast literature devoted to date to the rationale for and instructional aspects of "culture," there still exists a number of ambiguities suggesting that the task, though well begun, is far from completed. With respect to the first area, there is a general feeling that such cultural features as connotation, gestures, and so on, should be integrated in the materials considered the core of any given course. Though this aspiration is admirable and might be even more productive were the culture content of the core materials better structured, it reflects serious, inherent limitations.

Both the linguistic and situational level of any first-year program must of necessity be rudimentary if adjusted to the incremental task of learning the language. This is a crucial factor in determining the range and quality of cultural items integrated in the material. As a consequence, the "culture" content is often trivial (different kinds of windows), repetitive (the prototypical topic of wine, house, etc.), or limited (resulting in improper generalizations: *tu-vous* differentiation treated only partially to avoid exploring the full range of societal and emotional implications). The situation is further complicated if one insists on using the foreign language exclusively to draw sophisticated and significant inferences from the superficial data available from the usual text.

With respect to the second area, two tendencies are observable. Perhaps as an overreaction to previous notions of teaching culture, which, in many instances, consisted of ingurgitating "facts" related to history and geography, there is now great reluctance to consider any type of information based on the various disciplines and constituting the substance of political, economic, social, aesthetic, and intellectual history as significant to a truly "cultural" experience. It is seldom accepted that such "facts" can serve as a base for comparison and analysis, for setting current events and characteristics in a proper perspective, which, by a counterprocess, can generate as well as illuminate substantive problems.

The aversion to dealing with facts suggests substituting a problem-solving approach as appropriate in dealing with cultural concerns. The general merits of this approach are unquestionable, but again (and in great part as a result of limited language control) it is often used to probe the trivial rather than the significant. Often, elaborate simulations are set up to "discover" a cultural feature that could be described in a single sentence. The quarrel is not with the approach itself since, if it stimulates students, this is sufficient justification. We are merely concerned that, using the trivial feature as a given, it does not provide the starting point for serious inquiry that, by and large, would situate the external sign in the deeper, more significant cultural matrix of the society under consideration.[37]

The third area, because affect is more difficult to define and measure, is where the greatest breakdown in communication occurs and, as a result, the greatest amount of frustration prevails. Let us suppose that, under maximum conditions, we have provided the student with effective communication tools (language and gestures) and with a solid cognitive base that makes him knowledgeable about the mores of a country and the life-style of its people. What attitudes do we expect him to develop? How will this affect the way he functions in that culture? Will he increase his tolerance of differences and adjust his behavior only to the extent necessary to avoid confrontations or will he strive to internalize the foreign culture to the extent that he wishes to and becomes indistinguishable from a person native to the culture?

Given the difficulty of achieving total acculturation within the academic setting where direct immersion in the foreign culture is impractical, given our limited resources to approximate total immersion, the majority of students emerge with a broad tolerance for higher-order cultural differences but usually behave maladroitly at the functional level (verbal reactions, gestures, social graces). In my estimation this condition emerges from a significant paradox that has not been sufficiently assessed and to which we must turn our attention if many of our efforts in the teaching of culture are to remain productive.

We have a long tradition contributing to the image of the over-defensive American, self-conscious of his limited heritage, striving to make himself acceptable to the foreigner steeped in tradition and culture. In general, we may still be overdefensive in considering the way in which we are viewed by foreigners. Our present diffidence may be no more sophisticated than that indicated by the following quotation:

Just think for a minute what a drawback a bad accent is. He listens to you with something very much like contempt. You seem to him to be talking either like an ignorant man or like a child, and the association of ideas between a bad accent and ignorance or childishness is so close that he finds it practically impossible to treat you as he would an equal. Think what a pity that is, when it merely needs a thorough mastery of phonetics to put our children on an equal footing with the foreigner whose language they are learning.[38]

I submit that insisting on and magnifying our so-called

inadequacies and going to any length to become servile emulators serve not only to make us look ridiculous but, more significantly, to reinforce in our own minds the stereotype of the arrogantly intolerant foreigner.[39] To assume that the latter can accept, in a wide measure, the peculiarities of American culture may be doing him greater justice in terms of his own culture and of his human qualities. Mutual respect may indeed be more important than cultural transformation as means of achieving world unification.

Research

The need for basic research outlined by Dunkel in an earlier section (p. 10) was further specified by Carroll in Gage's *Handbook of Research on Teaching.*[40] Over the years Carroll has, while conducting significant research himself, been a constant advocate of more and better research as vital to the foreign-language field. This concern has been reflected in a corporate research effort mounted from a variety of perspectives. Periodic analysis of the logistics attending foreign-language instruction has been helpful in determining student enrollment, teacher availability, level of teacher competence, and other data important in making decisions and projections vital to the profession.[41] Independent of but related to foreign-language instruction, research has been continued and accelerated in such areas as verbal behavior, long- and short-span memory, and the relationship of many types of cognitive aptitudes to foreign-language learning.[42] Increasingly, the relationship of attitude to learning in general and to foreign-language learning in particular has become central to significant research efforts.[43]

Several major projects are representative of the profession's concern to evaluate the relative effectiveness of different methodologies and instructional strategies. These projects suffer the limitations attending most "action" research and are often suspect on the ground that important variables (teacher performance, relationship of teaching strategy to objectives) are treated in a somewhat cavalier fashion. More important, evaluation of student achievement as related to programs of instruction has proved generally disappointing in providing irrefutable documentation on a high level of proficiency reached in any skill area or the unequivocal superiority of one system of instruction over another. For instance, the Keating Report (1963) suggested that the language laboratory did not contribute significantly to more effective language learning. The Scherer-Wertheimer Report on the Denver Project (1964) pointed out rather conclusively that student performance was determined primarily by the objectives of the course intended to give priority to one skill as opposed to another. The more recent Pennsylvania Report (1969) "failed" to prove the superiority of the "functional" (audio-lingual) method over a more traditional approach. Though these negative findings have been hotly contested and, in some measure, convincingly refuted, the impact of the simplified "results" has contributed to the cynicism of the general public and caused justifiable concern in professional circles.[44]

A number of more modest efforts were aimed at determining the relative effectiveness of particular strategies (testing, drills, etc.).[45] Measurement of the impact of initiation to foreign languages in the grades on subsequent performance has also produced less than dramatic documentation.[46] In general, learning increment is usually reflected in relatively small percentages even in cases where, because of special treatment, it might be presumed that achievement would have doubled or trebled.[47]

While these efforts attest to the profession's concern for a data base as important to decision making, the results suggest that full benefits have not yet been realized. Much of the "pure" research in linguistics and psychology appearing in periodicals such as the *Journal of Educational Psychology*, the *Journal of Abnormal and Social Psychology*, the *Journal of Experimental Psychology*, and the *International Review of Applied Linguistics* is too specialized for the average teacher. In spite of the invaluable efforts of Carroll, Rivers, Pimsleur, Valdman, Politzer, Jakobovits, and others to function as mediators between theory and practice, many of the technical contributions of science are not yet synthesized to the point where they can be productively disseminated to the majority of practitioners.

Much of sophisticated research (on attitude, for instance) is often based on very special types of populations (e.g., anomie in French-speaking Maine), and the findings hold little promise of "transferability" to the typical heterogeneous group of students found in average classroom situations.

The limitation of research efforts to date may reflect either the paucity of foreign-language specialists trained in research methodology or their inability to address themselves to the "right" questions, those relating specifically to the teaching-learning quandaries that beset the schools. If such is the case, it speaks to a reorientation of at least a substantial part of subsequent research effort.

Quite independently of formal research, great strides were taken to develop standards of evaluation in the recent past. A serious attempt to assess various facets of foreign-language instruction resulted in the development of several types of evaluative measures.

Principally through the work of a number of committees supported by the Modern Language Association, several sets of "guidelines" were made available, setting both absolute and relative standards in such areas as teacher competence, teacher-preparation programs, course content, and levels of student achievement.[48]

More specifically in the field of measurement, handbooks were published to provide specific directions to teachers interested in using improved testing procedures to measure achievement in the several language skills. Note Lado's *Language Testing*[49] and, more recently, Valette's *Modern Language Testing*.[50] Valette also contributed a chapter on testing in foreign languages in *A Handbook on Formative and Summative Evaluation of Student Learning*. As the name implies, the latter compendium sets measurement in an evaluative context broader than that of previously available handbooks.[51]

Such important trends are reflected in the literature on testing in foreign languages. First, there has been a noted increase in concern for measuring the effect of instruction on students' attitudes[52] in addition to assessing accretion in the several language skills. Second, even at the cognitive level, more attention has been paid to development of the higher level skills than to mere recall of linguistic or cultural facts.[53] These new directions reflect the profession's concern for "accountability," best measured through the systematic development of specific behavioral objectives as they reflect individual performance in terms of "levels" of achievement rather than number of years of exposure.[54]

A number of normative tests has also been designed in the last decade: the Carroll and Sapon and Pimsleur prognosis tests; the MLA student achievement tests designed to cover four years of instruction at the secondary level; and the MLA Teacher Preparation Test covering seven areas of preparation including the areas of linguistic and professional preparation.[55] These various contributions have had a serious impact on professional thought and classroom practices. Critics of the various measuring instruments consider, as major limitations to current testing programs, some or all of the following:

1. Frequent failure to measure speaking skill on the grounds that it is a complex and time-consuming venture.
2. A certain bias on the part of test designers to overemphasize aspects of audio-lingual philosophy and content in test items.
3. Failure to include peripheral, nonsubject specific results ancillary to the teaching program.
4. Assessing measurement relative to achievement norms rather than as a point on an absolute continuum ranging from zero "native" proficiency.[56]

In spite of the above objections, testing is one of the areas in which foreign languages stand up well in contrast to the work of other subject-matter specialists in the generation preceding 1970. I shall return in more detail to the problem of evaluation and the implications for new directions in a subsequent chapter.

4 Educational and Professional Context

The Fickle Educational Climate

At the same time that international competition was dramatizing our national educational inadequacies, a strong case for a more stringent curriculum was being advocated in educational circles. Conant's *The Education of American Teachers*, though addressed specifically to the preparation of teachers, speaks clearly to the need of renewed emphasis on content, on the "solid" subjects as fundamental to serious improvement of curriculum at all levels. With respect to foreign languages he expresses his hope for a long, continuous sequence, preferably in the high school, as a requirement so important that, if it cannot be established in toto, should not be considered at all:

> In examining the high school program the reader will note that four years of a foreign language are specified, and here I would make one reservation. Unless the student has the ability to carry the study of language this far, and unless four years of instruction are offered in the high school, it might be better eliminated entirely. This is not a minor matter. The student who enters college with only two years of language training in high school, if he is to gain a proficiency, must devote at least two years of college to it. This time can ill be spared from the future teacher's program. The college years are too late for this job to be done. Therefore, *I suggest that until the secondary schools are regularly offering four consecutive years of language instruction, there is little point in giving language a fixed place in the requirements for "breadth" in the combined high school and college program.*[1]

But, by 1969, perhaps as manifestation of the ever-present seesaw struggle between educationists and subject-matter specialists, perhaps as a by-product of national crises imputed to

53

a failure on the part of the educational complex, we find ample evidence that curriculum orientation has been radically changed.[2] The charge against traditionalism is made specific:

The subject matter departments, finally, have failed American education in that they have not provided the American education exactly what they have demanded that American education provide for them—that is, people who are intellectually competent. The subject matter departments have been primarily in control of the curriculum reforms of the last decade; yet, in a survey I did of mathematics, social sciences, English and other subjects, I found that only about 15 per cent of the subject matter departments has met the demands that they made as curriculum builders.[3]

The literature is explicit as to the kind of intellectual competence required in the present age. It emphasizes criteria for developing a new citizenry capable of coping in a world seemingly committed to tearing itself apart.

The scope of and reason for discontent is elaborated as follows: Perhaps a more telling criticism argues that emphasis upon conceptual content and methods of the disciplines is no guarantee that the basic questions that concern man will be confronted. What is the purpose of man's struggle on earth? Why should anyone attempt to find his niche in a bureaucratic society and prepare himself to make good in it? Why attempt to follow the established social and political procedures when they do not seem to lead to the goals which are promised? What is the point of trying to make good in a world that seems bent upon self-destruction? These are the kinds of questions which most, if not all, the disciplines seem to neglect. Perhaps it is not the lack of some all-embracing unity that impoverishes the educational program. Perhaps it is the failure of discipline-oriented education to confront with intellectual refinement and integrity the basic value issues of the modern world.[4]

In this real world, real students have a right to ask real questions. These are predicated on the criterion of utility and focus on the problem of individual and social survival.

The teacher is constantly asked: "Why should I learn that?" "What is the use of studying history?" "Why should I be required to take biology?" If the intent of these questions is to ask what use

can one make of them in everyday activities, only general answers
are possible. We can and do talk about the relevance of subject
matter to the decisions and activities that pupils will have to
make. We know, among other things, that they must:
———choose and follow a vocation,
———exercise the tasks of citizenship,
———engage in personal relationships,
———take part in culture-carrying activities.[5]

The arguments summarized above may be thought as extreme
by some and iconoclastic by others. It must be noted, however,
that, in principle, they reflect the position of the same Office of
Education that, ten years before, had propagandized for
increasing enrollment in foreign-language classes.

We are not sure where the "new" curriculum will be leading
us, but there is no doubt as to how far the pendulum has swung.
The concept that second-language mastery is the "hallmark of an
educated man," the elitist approach, the pursuit of studies
because of their respective inherent values, the stability of
foreign-language offerings required by faculties as a legitimate
prescription contributing to "general" education, most of the
long-standing props underpinning the curriculum structure are
reviled in no uncertain terms.

For, even if the four general categories for determining utility
listed above (choose and follow a vocation, etc.) are applicable
each in different and somewhat minimal measure to the scrutiny
of the long process in foreign-language accretion, they may be
more "relevant" to developing sensitivity to another culture than
to an extended period of study dedicated to the mastering of
language skills. Furthermore, it is difficult to assess the degree to
which students will be aware of the appropriateness of foreign-
language study as instrumental to meeting the needs suggested by
the above categories.

Besides the major shift outlined above, several other
important trends in "education" took place that, in various
degrees, had implications for foreign-language instruction.

The educational enterprise became generally concerned with
the so-called discovery approach to learning, with the nurturing
of inquiry techniques, in short, with process rather than content.

By inference, this thrust relegated to a level of secondary importance the accretion of knowledge (facts) and the investment of time in activities that involved mainly recall through rote-learning. It is not difficult to see how foreign languages, if narrowly defined as a discipline and if represented by the mim-mem activities associated with "overlearning to the point of automaticity," could be integrated with difficulty into Bruner's concept of education.[6]

At a broader level, the concentration on better methodologies focusing entirely on subject matter tended to isolate foreign-language instruction in the eyes of curriculum specialists increasingly concerned with adapting new models to the total school experience as integral to personality development and providing new tools essential to survival in an environment changing at a vertiginous pace. And indeed, we find foreign languages, in spite of the dramatic internal ferment evident in the 50s, treated casually as a curriculum movement by Goodlad in his *School Curriculum Reform*.[7]

Concomitant to these general directions might be cited the trend away from a teacher-centered to a child-centered style of instruction (as measured by Flander's analysis techniques, for instance),[8] the insistence on accountability by measuring results not only on the cognitive but, perhaps more importantly, on an affective scale, and a renewed commitment of the school to teach all children, regardless of previous academic experience, basic talent, or background.

I shall attempt to develop in a later section the response of the foreign-language profession to the above and other educational trends such as team teaching, modular scheduling, differentiated staff, and individualized instruction. For the present, it may be sufficient to point out that foreign-language methodologists, preoccupied with a serious survival problem, reflecting a long tradition of elitism, by definition committed to content orientation, more or less forced into a position of insularity by the nature of the subject and by cultural heritage, were not able or did not choose to cope with the ferment surging around them, at least to the satisfaction of the noncommitted and critical.

Erosion

The Office of Education through its support to pre-service and in-service training had recognized the importance of the teacher's function in transforming "New Key" precepts into practices affecting the students in classrooms across the land. As an index of the success of this particular thrust, note the case of "Mlle Colombe" (circa 1964).[9]

Mlle Colombe had taught French for a good many years and was deservedly considered a "master teacher." She possessed those characteristics that generate enthusiasm in a class; stubborn dedication to her task inspired maximum effort on the part of each student. She had worked under good men in a better than average university. She was active in the organization of the school where she taught. Mlle Colombe was loved, respected, and reasonably happy.

Complacency was not one of Mlle Colombe's shortcomings. Years of what she considered moderate success had not blunted her sensitivity to a changing world, its current needs, the tenor of new trends. She was determined to keep informed. She religiously attended meetings, workshops, conferences. She read as much as time allowed.

Mlle Colombe could remember "hard" times. And the initial impetus was far from spent. Mlle Colombe was awed by the contagious quality of urgent, visionary messages constantly projecting ever-better techniques and the potential of unexploited media.

A time came when she could not be content with simply pledging allegiance to the cause. Wanting to be actively involved in the exciting national venture, she felt it imperative to work out her own adjustment to the "New Key." She had no illusions as to the magnitude of the task involved in catching up and keeping up with new theories and practices. Secure in her past achievements and fired by a wonderfully new enthusiasm, she set out vigorously and optimistically to achieve her conversion.

She realized that, given the impact of linguistics on foreign-language teaching, she needed to increase her knowledge in this area. It was with anticipation that she turned her attention to a field that she had had no opportunity to investigate during her formal education.

Since Mlle Colombe's period of self-instruction anteceded the publication of the *Linguistic Reading Lists*, her reading was somewhat desultory.[10] Nevertheless, she was elated at first by a feeling of making good progress.

It was perhaps unfortunate that as she pursued her investigation she had prematurely tackled Joseph H. Greenberg's *Essay in Linguistics*.[11] Assuming that the "difficulty" of linguistics was being compounded by a lack of familiarity with mathematics, she began to doubt that her resources in terms of time and background would ever permit her to grasp the subject in depth.

Eventually, remembering the following injunction from Fries's *Structure of English* helped assuage her distress.

Too often, it is true, the linguistic materials upon which teachers should build are presented in a form and in a language quite specialized and remote from that of educated laymen. Perhaps the solution is for more teachers to try to understand the scientific work in linguistics and for more linguists to try to write so that they may be more widely understood.[12]

But, in the last analysis, it was of little comfort to her that linguists themselves deplored their incapacity to communicate at a subtechnical level, and the following passage did little to alleviate her frustration:

Granted that there can be rational justification for the antiscientific attitude it has not been helped by either the style or the content of much recent linguistic writing. From the chaotic algebras of Zellig Harris's *Methods in Structural Linguistics* through the latest tortured exegesis on the Transformational revolution, too many linguists have used their claim to scientific precision as an excuse for being incomprehensible to all save the trebly-baptized of their private cliques.[13]

Finally, Mlle Colombe had to resign herself to the observation that:

As a scientist the linguist is searching for pure knowledge. To know the facts and to understand the language processes are to him ends in themselves. He usually leaves to others the business of applying practically the knowledge he has won.[14]

It was fortunate that in a period of discouragement she could divert her effort to the intermediary role of increasing importance being played by the applied linguists, a group dedicated to "interpret" pure science in such a way as to make it functional for the practitioner. Mlle Colombe found that, as a result of her previous browsing, she could cope comfortably with the latter group, and that articles in the journals pointed the way for translating linguistic principles into effective classroom procedures. Mlle Colombe was reassured as she saw that the gaps between pure theory and functional practices were being prudently minimized.[15]

There were instances, however, when she did not quite understand how certain linguistic generalizations had come to be translated into concrete formulations by the applied branch of the confrérie. She had no difficulty accepting the linguist's interest in the spoken language as the prime mode of communication, but she was not so clear as to the ineluctable logic that prescribed the dialogue as the exemplary vehicle for teaching the spoken language. Though she understood the scientific concern for impartial observation of structures as they spontaneously occurred without thought of controlling vocabulary or modifying normal speed of delivery, she was not convinced that concessions were not necessary at the instructional level: selection of patterns on the basis of relative complexity, of vocabulary on the basis of "frequency" and topical interest. She rather suspected that relentlessly exposing a class to utterances delivered at conversational speed was character-building for the better students and, unfortunately, mystifying for others.

She readily accepted language as "becoming increasingly valuable to the scientific study of a given culture" and as "a guide to 'social reality.'" On the basis of her experience, however, she had doubts concerning the potency of the "cultural island" or of participation in a culturally significant action as an antidote to limited aptitude and to the observable depression often detectable in students for whom, for whatever reasons, the foreign-language experience seemed uncongenial.

As a whole, she learned her lesson well, became fluent in the new nomenclature, talked of structures, taught through the use of pattern drills, concentrated her efforts on areas of interference, tried to shy away from "translation," seldom referred to "vocabulary," and never exposed her students to word lists. Two areas of transitions were extremely easy to span: She had rarely used English in her class; her room, from the point of view of "cultural" decor, had always been the envy of her colleagues.

Mlle Colombe was open-minded about electronics. At least, she thought, the field could not be ignored. She had no real aptitude for mechanics but, on the other hand, she was not prone to phobia of gadgetry and found ridiculous the unnecessary palliative in the commercial blurbs to the effect that "the machine will never replace the teacher." Uninhibited by fear for her status and by concern for the machine as a shrinker of children's heads, she made amazing strides. Helped by the works of such experts as Holton, Marty, and Stack,[16] she became quickly conversant with the audio and visual media, their purpose, assets, and limitations. She did not yet have a laboratory at her disposal, but she testified enthusiastically to the effectiveness of the listening posts installed along one wall of her classroom.

As she began to feel comfortable with her competence in the areas of linguistics and electronics, Mlle Colombe felt a strong compulsion to incorporate her findings into the French sequence at her school. Since she envisioned some rather drastic changes, she wished to do this rationally, gradually, even cautiously. Not altogether confident in the effectiveness of her do-it-yourself activities, she seriously considered attending a summer institute, thereby confirming her direction and stamping her efforts with official approval. She decided against it, partly because she had long promised herself a summer in Europe, partly because she convinced herself that, given the plethora of resources available, this would not be essential to her projects.

The materials that Mlle Colombe adopted for her "new

course" lived up to the claims of the designers in many ways. Initially they were well received by the students, some of whom maintained a high level of enthusiasm throughout the year and, as a result, reached a high level of achievement in hearing and speaking.

Mlle Colombe shared her students' enthusiasm. She was veritably indefatigable in the matter of substitution drills and became increasingly appreciative of her "listening posts" as they worked tirelessly to ensure memorization of dialogues to the desired point of automaticity.

At the beginning, she had had grave concern for three of her students who were apparently handicapped by some not-so-obvious aural deficiency. She thought of their forbearance as comparable to that of the blind at a silent-film festival.

Periodically she had moments of impatience and apprehension. The whole process was thorough but incredibly time-consuming—at least to one conditioned by years of experience to move at a rather brisk pace through a sizable body of material. As spring approached, she intuitively sensed certain resistances to the dialogues that constituted the core of new material. The students seemed to have increasing difficulty (or reluctance) in memorizing them. In a rather desperate mood she began, after a short audio-lingual presentation, to work out the dialogues with the aid of a script distributed to the students. She was relieved when a few weeks later she received the long-awaited *Teacher's Guide* and found her procedure was "permissible" under certain emergency conditions.

During the spring quarter serious gaps between the level of achievement of different students became obvious, and consequent differences in the degree of motivation of respective students became evident. The more "intellectual" types began either to demand some outlet commensurate to their capacities or to fall into a state verging on apathy. Mlle Colombe, somewhat desperate, found herself unconsciously falling back on her area of greatest strength. Grammatical explanations became a routine part of each class session.

At the years's end Mlle Colombe had opportunity to reflect on her venture. She was still completely convinced of its inherent merits. Whatever limitations she had observed were, she thought, due as much to her incapacities, lack of proper training, and lack of faith as they were to the "system."

Many times during this period of transition Mlle Colombe felt guilty for her eclecticism and desolate in her isolation. She saw herself wedged inextricably between the demands of theory and practice, between her aspirations and her capacity for fulfilling them. Much later, articles such as Max Zeldner's "The Bewildered Modern Language Teacher"[17] and Theodore Huebener's "The New Key Is Now Off-Key"[18] formulated what heretofore had been cautious allusions, camouflaged reservations exchanged in an atmosphere of conspiracy by teachers seeking mutual support. Mlle Colombe reflected somberly that hers was not an isolated case, that the debilitating malaise to which she was a prey, the attending symptoms of insecurity, apprehension, deterioration of confidence were decreasing the effectiveness of teachers in many classrooms and in several subject areas.

The fact that she was making progress, that she was becoming increasingly knowledgeable, was little comfort.

She was still anxious to assimilate the impressive diet of literature coming from an ever-increasing number of directions, to translate it in such a responsible way as to make it efficiently operative within her classroom. But this ambitious attitude served only to make her increasingly conscious of the insufficiency of time, knowledge, and energy at her disposal.

Her morale was at its lowest when her efforts did not result in the anticipated reaction and achievement among the students in her class. In a particularly pessimistic mood, Mlle Colombe wondered if this distress was not peculiar to her field. Would not her task have been easier in an area where cumulative progress was less important and brute rote-learning less essential? She thought wistfully of her more fortunate colleagues teaching in subject areas where motivation was self-generating, stimulating young minds in the ways of inquiry, or nurturing fragile buds of creativity through a series of meaningful experiences.

She had long made a distinction between rote-learning and

rote-teaching, and she was convinced that rote-learning (the memorizing essential in the early stages of language-learning) was central to the problem of motivation. She sensed that a direct attempt to minimize the burden of memorization was indicated. Essentially, this involved shortening the amount of time and reducing the amount of effort invested between the period of initial enthusiasm and a necessarily remote reward. In a vague, intuitive way she became increasingly convinced that if students could be directed to memorize more material faster with greater resulting retention, if their full capacity for analogizing could be systematically developed, progress might be accelerated to such an extent that a high level of motivation might be more easily sustained.

Wilga M. Rivers's *The Psychologist and the Foreign-Language Teacher* answered some of her questions but left her still very much perplexed by the complications that the "New Key" had superimposed on the already nebulous area of memorization.[19] The audio-lingual approach emphasized learning through hearing (a sense not usually linked with verbal-learning investigations), de-emphasized grammar (thus reducing the possibility of using an "organizer"), and eliminated written translation (long a prop for establishing representational equivalence).

Although Mlle Colombe envisaged controls in the classroom situation and controls in the structuring and sequencing of materials, although she dreamed of materials and techniques that might indeed produce miraculous results, she felt helpless, since she was not sufficiently specialized to outline the basic principles on which such controls would be predicated in order to hold at least a promise of success.

Wistfully, Mlle Colombe realized that her explorations had qualified her to teach better but that she was not yet prepared to teach how to learn. She felt no rancor that the promise of linguistics, electronics, and psychology remained largely unfulfilled, that though the message had reached the teacher it had hardly begun to affect the child. She anticipated the day when a consorted thrust by the various disciplines would provide her with more appropriate tools.

In the meantime, she would simply do the best she could.

Part Two   Prospect

5 Back to the Drawing Board

The Changing Scene

The contrasts between the foreign-language scene in 1960 and 1970 are striking. The apogee of the audio-lingual method in the 60s was marked by support from the general public, substantial backing by government finances, and a benevolent educational climate. Student enrollment was on the increase and, consequently, teachers were in demand. A combination of these factors resulted in corporate optimism and professional élan.

In contrast, by 1970, professionals increasingly contest the theoretical base of the audio-lingual method and deplore the lack of documentation concerning its effectiveness. The public is questioning the values of formal education, particularly the "traditional" subjects. Government is investing its resources in new "higher priority" areas. Educational theorists are reacting against those subjects that are not instrumental in maximizing psychological and social development. Students are questioning the "relevance" of foreign-language study.

In short, every foreign-language teacher is sensitive in some measure to shortage of funds, shortage of students, oversupply of teachers, lack of a cohesive instructional rallying point, disenchantment with panaceas. Elan has been replaced with malaise, optimism with apprehension.

And yet, paradoxically, the external reasons adduced for foreign-language study are still as viable today as they were a decade ago. Bilingualism (in whatever measure) is still considered by many as a valuable asset; removal of language barriers is still considered essential to international communication in commerce and politics; the world as a result of improved communication and transportation is still shrinking increasingly.

Given the consistency of external factors, it is my intent to concentrate in this second section on such internal considerations as need to be updated in terms of the current situation. In doing so, I shall try to proceed from simple observations as opposed to predicating my thesis on broad generalizations. I shall try to develop an argument based on student reactions rather than theory. I shall start from the situation as it is rather than what it should be or might have been.

We observe that enrollment is down, that it may further decrease in the future. We postulate that as long as any number of students, for whatever reason (practical or esoteric), is vaguely interested in any foreign language it is incumbent on the educational enterprise to provide programs for these students. We predict that if such programs are restructured to meet student needs, if they are beneficial rather than discouraging, elective rather than imposed, a new trend in increased enrollment will occur. In short, given a nucleus of students with a "neutral" set, we submit that the focus needs to be less on increasing the number of enrollees than on maintaining the interest of whatever numbers are enrolled as prerequisite to expanding our field of influence.

To this end I shall express my own notions of what is required. It is my opinion, and that of other colleagues, that any program must produce demonstrable results (direct or tangential), that the process of instruction must be enjoyable as well as productive, that it must fit somewhere in the matrix of intellectual growth. More importantly, I shall take the position that, for the individual learner, some kind of immediate success is as important as the prospect of long-range reward and that this kind of success can only be achieved by each according to his talents, predilections, and social condition.

I shall not hesitate to draw from the legacy of the last generation. Nor shall I be reluctant to draw from my personal experience in the elementary, secondary, and college classroom during these past, too-many years. For it is from this experience that I conclude that instruction could be better focused, that eventual reactions to the "long sequence," to the total spectrum of foreign instruction, is determined by the student's perception of what happens to him in the initial phase, the first year, perhaps the first week of exposure.

When the Lights Go Out

The class of beginners on the first day of school is usually characterized by curious, eager faces, general attentiveness, and a high level of participation. Unfortunately, when we look at the same group six months, a year, or two years later, it is hardly recognizable. Among those that remain, few are enthusiastic, many are scarcely tolerant, some are resigned and apathetic, too many verge on being disruptive.

Sensitive teachers are saddened by this turn of events. They sometimes assume personal responsibility for the deterioration and, in their discouragement, seek more overtly rewarding professional occupations. More often, they reach for facile excuses. It is either the children, who are lazy, anti-intellectual, or immature, or the subject, which is inherently difficult, boring, or too cumulative, or the method, which is dull and repetitious, or the content, which is stupid and irrelevant. Most bemoan the fact that the situation is at best artificial, that there is neither need nor opportunity to use the foreign language as a functional tool immediately related to reality in the context of life experiences.

And certainly, in some measure and at different times, all of these negative forces do affect the climate of a class. Notwithstanding, let us indulge briefly in a bit of fantasy in order to be more specific as to when and how the morale of the group decays.

Let us imagine that our vaunted technology made it possible to connect each child's mind to a light bulb: when the child's mind is working the bulb burns bright; when the child tunes out, the bulb goes out.

At the beginning of the language sequence we would expect the entire panel of lights for the class to be turned on. Some time later, a number of lights would be extinguished. At a much later date, only a few sporadic lights would pervade the depressing darkness of the classroom.

But the electric hookup (if we had it) would provide us with much more than these periodic checks into the intellectual efforts of the group. More important, they would give us a cue as to individual responses at any given time and to any given activity in the class.

John's light, for instance, would burn brightly as he listened and understood, but would turn off when he was asked to respond.

Mary's light would be on all through a repetition drill but would turn off whenever she was asked to dramatize a part in the dialogue.

Joseph's light would be off generally—except when he tried to write in his notebook some phonetic approximation of what he was hearing.

The light system would make us very much aware of what each child responded to, what he liked, what he was good at—what turned him on and what tuned him out.

It would furthermore enable us to observe—and record, if we wished—that John's light, typically, remained on for a long time, turned off briefly, and then came on again. It would give us a basis for relating John's light signals to the class activities. More generally, we might observe that the individual lights seldom went out suddenly, never to go on again. Instead, we would probably discern a pattern: each light would tend to go out with increasing frequency for increasingly longer periods of time.

Such a system, if we had it, would afford us a precious set of signals. Knowing that John's light had just gone out, we could try to find out why, to work with him in such a way that his light would go back on as soon as possible. We would probably also notice that the sooner his light was turned back on, the longer the interval before the next period of darkness.

But we do not have such a system and probably, as far as classroom use, will not have it in the near future.

So teachers do the best they can. Through intuition and experience, preferably through a combination of both, they sense that some lights are on and some are off. And they try to cope. They vary activities, quicken the pace. They compliment or scold. They review or go faster. They hope that by some strategy involving the entire class they can manage to keep the greatest number of lights turned on most of the time.

Sometimes, if the teacher is extremely perceptive, well trained, and completely composed, he or she has opportunity to diagnose what part of the massive corpus of material that the class is working with is particularly hard for Mary or which learning style is most congenial to John. And indeed, when this happens, Mary and John respond positively.

In the present state of the art and science of foreign-language teaching several factors militate against diagnosing and responding to individual differences of students' attitudes and aptitudes.
A. The total sequence and the component courses are considered in global terms. The terminal goal of bilingualism punctuated at various levels of "proficiency" is pursued in a nondifferentiated way: all parts are assumed to contribute vaguely to the whole. Though justified in part by the admittedly cumulative aspects of foreign-language learning, this process tends to violate any precept leading to individualized instruction. At worst, it is characterized by servile and relentless adherence to the syllabus. At best it results in futile attempts to "adjust" activities in order to cope with initial and continuing differences in the quantity and quality of the learning taking place. This adjustment, a relatively simple matter at the beginning of the sequence, becomes increasingly difficult as the materials accumulate. Beyond a certain point, diagnosis of specific areas of strength and weaknesses becomes impossible, the causes buried somewhere in the total corpus of material previously covered. The "A" student represents a child who, somehow, is a good all-around student. The "F" student is one who, some place along the way, fell off the wagon. Short of any refined instrumentality for coping with these obvious gaps in performance the teacher plows onward aiming at the "middle of the class" with some dissolute attempt to provide random enrichment for the bored high achiever and usually futile "special work" for the by now defeated and recalcitrant nonachiever.
B. The system of instruction is generally conceived in linear terms.
   Whatever the long-range and immediate goals of in-

struction, whether the course is designed for mastery of all skills or of some particular skill, these are attacked in a continuing, nondeviating forward direction for all students. The occasional "review" constitutes a look backward over the straight path covered. There is little if any opportunity for individual bifurcation and detour. Either alternate paths are closed off as inappropriate to the goals of the course or students are not allowed to indulge themselves in productive delays since this interferes with the single-tract momentum of the group. Regardless of the student's talent for mimicry, he may perfect or improve his accent only within the time prescribed for the total learning task set for the group. A student with limited aural acuity has no opportunity to master the writing system as a prerequisite for memorization if this infringes on his being exposed, "on schedule," to the incomprehensible tapes allegedly prepared for that purpose.

The linear approach has dire consequences insofar as it violates any consideration for differentiated aptitudes. In many cases it fails to exploit the individual's "readiness" for a particular aspect of foreign-language learning. Most often it commits students to move from questionable success to failure rather than allowing him to develop an area of strength in order to move with confidence to a skill for which he is less gifted.

C. The orientation of instruction is generally unidirectional.

Historically, foreign-language instruction has reflected domination by some often-justified, sometimes doctrinaire, pedagogical point of view. Enough has been written about the relative superiority (generally undocumented) of one method over another. The usual adverse reaction in some quarters to each of these methods, the tendency on the part of the teacher to "help" the method, which leads to a variety of eclectic approaches, is perhaps based on a sound analysis of student reactions as much as a matter of personal caprice. It seems unlikely indeed that within a certain epoch all students should respond with equal enthusiasm, competence, and success to an intellectualized approach to foreign-language learning but that, in a subsequent decade, an equally representative student population should be universally responsive to mim-mem exposure.

It is probably neither irreverent nor cynical to propose that no single method, no single corpus of material may be appropriate to individualizing teaching and learning in any given situation.

The Instructional Module

The present systems of instructional materials and practices, insofar as they inherently reduce the possibility of individualizing instruction, lead us to search for a program that is not restrictive because of its global, linear, and unidirectional approach. We shall call this approach a *modular* approach. It is characterized by the following features.

A. The module becomes the core of instruction. It is a discrete unit made up of limited vocabulary and structures selected on some organizational basis such as frequency, utility, or pedagogical expediency. Any language skill or subskill appropriate to the module can be taught to the point of mastery. The course, and eventually the sequence, is made up of a number of such integrated, clearly identified modules. Because of the discrete nature of each module, diagnosis, appropriate instructional strategies, and evaluation can be much more specific with consequent increase in participation on the part of the student.

B. Each module can be attacked from several angles. The limited repertoire involved in the module permits easy fragmentation in language skills and subskills that can be taught in connection with a particular module. Ready diagnosis of what skill or subskill is most appropriate to each student's aptitudes permits a nonlinear progression. For example, a student receptive to purely audio-lingual work might proceed through a series of modules limiting his activities to that approach while another student, intent on learning to write, might master writing the materials contained in the same series without concern for memorizing the content. It is the intent of the system that, at some appropriate point, each student should extend his special skill to other skills, which he had neglected in previous modules making up the series. At any point in the learning continuum a student can be profiled to indicate his level of mastery across modules horizontally and across component skills and subskills vertically.

C. The modular system provides for a multidirectional teaching and learning system.

As has been mentioned, the discrete feature of the module facilitates teacher assessment and student self-diagnosis permitting immediate identification of areas of strength and preference. The area or areas on which the student concentrates is not determined by "theory" but rather by the degree of success that the student encounters in meeting goals of his own selection. The decision to move from a linear one-skill to an epicyclic all-skills approach is a joint decision between the student and the teacher.

The teacher's task and effectiveness as a diagnostician and instructor is facilitated by the discreteness of the individual module as further fragmented into skill and subskill components. He can evaluate individual progress, plan transitions, and arrive at more systematic decisions concerning instructional strategies, selection of appropriate media, and general counseling since he can, at any point, estimate the student's total progress in terms of one or several skills. He is further challenged to devise new strategies and interventions for facilitating transfer from one skill to another within the same module.

D. Each module, in addition to providing opportunity for concentrating on clearly differentiated skills and subskills, must also provide flexibility in the way these skills, independently or in combination, are attacked. Students with different learning styles, for instance, may opt for different ways of "memorizing" a dialogue. One may feel comfortable learning it by repeating after a model to the point of mastery. Another may wish to learn the component vocabulary before assembling the total context. One may decide to proceed from structure drills to generalizations; another may wish to start with an abstract "rule" and apply it to the lexical repertoire under control. The more cautious student may see "free expression" as the culmination of drills appropriate to the module while the more venturesome may consider the confrontation with "free expression" as a stimulus for developing the prerequisite skills.

The teacher faced with any corpus of language material involving X lexical and Y structural items (a module) must be aware of the opportunity for selecting and teaching a number of skills and subskills in the context of that material. The following checklist is fairly typical of the directions that skill-development might take. It has already been mentioned that fragmentation of the language unit permits greater specificity in goal setting with consequent increase in the possibility of measuring and recording individual achievement in behavioral terms.

The following list of subskills reflects my own pedagogical bias rather than consonance with psychological or linguistic tenets. It is not proposed as the only way of looking at foreign-language learning but rather as a tentative attempt to view the process systematically. It may be noted that I distinguish between "passive" and "active" language behavior and stress heavily the importance of recall as a prerequisite to speaking and writing. As complex as is this cognitive function I feel that, in spite of its importance, it has been treated in a cavalier fashion in the recent past. Too often it has been assumed that it will take place. Vaguely implied in the slogan "learning to the point of auto-maticity," memorization has been insufficiently investigated as central to spoken or written expression.

Chart 2 points to the variety of skills and subskills that can be attained singly or in combination with each other.

It is to be emphasized that the set of objectives shown in chart 2, applicable to the total language sequence, is intended to be viewed specifically in terms of a discrete module. Limiting application to a specified linguistic repertoire facilitates the "learning" of the objective to the point of mastery. It is feasible to measure specifically whether or not the student can recall ten stems, can spell them as well (including the addition of

CHART 2

Aural Understanding
The student can
A. discriminate among auditory cues
B. identify signals provided by
   1. stems
   2. morphological segments
   3. syntactical features
   4. intonational features
C. identify subcomponents
D. conceptualize the total message
   in terms of the above information

Speaking
The student can
A. produce all necessary
   phonemes correctly
B. recall appropriate
   1. stems
   2. morphological segments
   3. syntactical signals
C. produce the total message
   1. with proper breath groups
   2. with proper stress
      characteristics
   3. with proper intonation
   4. with reasonable "flow"

Reading
A. Oral Reading*
The student can
   1. Produce the phoneme
      corresponding to
      a. single letters
      b. letter combination
      c. anomalies
      d. diacritical modification
   2. read aloud the total message
      a. with proper breath groups
      b. with proper stress
         characteristics
      c. with proper intonation
      d. without undue "stoppage"
B. Context Reading
The student can

1. identify the signals provided by
   a. stems
   b. morphological segments
   c. syntetical features
   d. diacritical signals
   e. punctuation marks
2. identify subcomponents of the
   total message
3. conceptualize the total message
   in terms of the above
   information

*Writing**
A. Spelling
The student can spell correctly
   1. on the basis of oral
      repertoire (or recall)
      a. single letters reflecting
         phonemic-graphemic
         correspondence
      b. letter combinations
         reflecting phomemic-
         graphemic correspondence
   2. on the basis of recall
      a. silent letters
      b. anomalies
      c. diacritical signs
      d. morphological segments
      e. punctuation marks
B. Composition
The student can
   1. recall appropriate
      a. stems
      b. morphological segments
      c. syntactical devices
   2. organize subcomponents of
      total message
   3. relate components of total
      message to each other
   4. produce total message in
      writing at reasonable
      speed

*In the case of several languages (e.g., Russian, Greek) calligraphy constitutes
an additional subskill.

"s" for the plural), or can write a coherent sentence based on the limited material available. Progress and problems are more easily identified than they can be in a "course" where the nature and causes of deficiencies tend to be blurred by the interrelated and cumulative process of instruction.

Fragmentation of the learning task also permits clearer notions as to what specific subskill is to be attacked in a given period. Obviously, all subskills cannot be taught in a 40-to-50 minute span. Systematic analysis of performance on the more complex objectives should suggest points of attack for remediation on the subobjectives leading to a previous failure. To achieve "reasonable flow" in speaking suggests looking for clues of a breakdown, possibly at as low a level as "recall of stems."

Clear identification of tasks (subskills) involved in the mastery of a single skill helps us to visualize that a progression from simple to complex is not always necessary. For some students, it might be easier to achieve fluency in speaking by memorizing a set of utterances (dialogue). For others, the inverse process of building up the dialogue by drilling on the components might be more congenial. For a third category, combining these activities might prove more productive.

A schema of detailed objectives is also helpful in determining the point at which a multiskill approach might be most effective. A single word, for instance, can provide focus for recall and phonemic production (speaking), for establishing graphemic-phonemic correspondence, for stem identification (reading) and correct spelling (writing). It may be noted again that the sequence of the process again may be reversed (writing-reading-speaking) through simultaneous audiovisual presentation.

The above obviously implies confidence in the usefulness of clarifying behavioral objectives. It may be suggested, however, that while each general objective might be further refined by producing a single, valid test item, it is perhaps more productive to consider each general objective as generating a set of appropriate activities related to teacher input, student activity, and adequate resources. In order for a student to demonstrate a given behavior the teacher has the responsibility of meeting required instructional behavior, structuring productive student activities, and providing the necessary functional resources. Too often, the teacher's responsibility, competence, and obligations are assumed, and instruction consists more of pious exhortations or threats than systematic contributions to aid in the mastering of the intended goals.

Chart 3 illustrates a few ways in which this generative process operates.

The obvious application of the system outlined in Chart 3 is the designing of a complete, systematic branched program in which the lexical and structural parameters are carefully controlled and sequenced, in which instructional strategies are carefully described, and for which adequate audiovisual resources are provided.

Pending development and marketing of such a program the essential features of the system provide some orientation to the teacher in terms of reconceptualizing the instructional task in the direction of greater individualization. The principles of delineating a discrete area (fragmenting the limited corpus of material in terms of skills and subskills and allowing students to operate initially from an area of strength) can serve in the adaptation of any textbook or basal materials prescribed for the course. This attempt at systematizing eclecticism is considered vital to more precise diagnosis, to more appropriate instructional strategies, and to more realistic and accurate evaluation. Such adaptations should stimulate student involvement and sustain motivation by enabling the student to operate consistently at a high level commensurate with his aptitude through such activities as are most congenial to his style of learning.

The approach also suggests guidelines to achieving flexibility in teaching strategies in contrast to attacking a series of "units" through identical repetition activities (memorization and/or drill, for instance). The number of skills and subskills previously outlined suggests a practically infinite number of ways by which, singly, in combination, or in different sequences, any corpus of material can provide the basis for varied activities selected as appropriate to individual students at any particular time. This should help to reduce the tedium often associated with foreign-

CHART 3

(Student demonstrates competence in the area of . . .)	Teacher Input (Teacher assumes responsibility for adequate . . .)	Student Activity (Teacher structures activities that involve student . . .)	Resources (Teacher insures availability of . . .)
Phonation	Acoustical description	Repeat dialogue	Laboratory
Aural discrimination	Acoustical description	Matched pair drill	Record and test sheet
Aural comprehension	Explication of context	Listening to text	Movie clip
Recall (vocabulary)	Association with concept	Multisensory drill	Flash cards and tape recorder
Recall (structure)	Explication	Pattern drill	Laboratory
Spelling	Description of correspondence	Systematic association drill	Workbook
Oral reading	Description of correspondence	Systematic association drill	"Voice Master"
Oral reading	Discussion of semantic-structural correspondence	Identify breath groups	Transparencies
Composition	Review of component parts	Write "composition"	Series of visual cues

language instruction as it affects both students and teachers.

Analysis of the skills and subskills also points to planning strategies amd structuring evaluation in two distinct directions. It is evident that a number of objectives are finite in the sense that the task is limited and that "mastery" can be achieved in a predictable length of time. Given the limited number of phonemes, it can be assumed that, for each student, maximum capacity to discriminate or to pronounce correctly can be determined at a given point in time. The same principle applies, in general, to oral reading and to many of the subskills involved in writing and speaking. On the other hand, any activity related to recall (particularly of stems and anomalies) suggests the same process for the foreign-language student as for the native speaker. Such considerations suggest the possibility of systematically "mastering" a number of subskills to the point where they are no longer a problem of interference as the student increases his competence. This also suggests greater emphasis on process than on accumulating content, that is, focusing primarily on vocabularly accretion and syntactic control without serious concern for the process of utilizing content in a creditable and legitimate language activity. It is not uncommon, for instance, to find even third-year students reading haltingly from a text, without concern for breath groups, stress, and intonation. Having been insufficiently alerted to and drilled in the process of correct reading habits in the early stages of instruction they carry their disability along throughout their language experience. The same applies to "fluency" as characterized by "reasonable flow" or of "deciphering" words in a written text without grasping the total context.

It is my position that correct habituation can be developed in the early stages by concentration on an individual skill and insisting on perfecting process rather than cumulating content and that, furthermore, the focus on any specific skill is uncomplicated by problems emerging from superimposition of incompetence in other skills. Improper oral reading, for instance, may be as much a function of struggling with meaning (context reading) as with making proper graphemic-phonemic associations (in the sphere of oral reading).

approach, a different program. The fact that they elaborate my own convictions may give the impression that I am indeed proposing another panacea as alternate to those previously adulated. In fact, I realize that I am not proposing even an entirely original point of view. I am suggesting a shift in emphasis rather than an "innovative" doctrine. I am suggesting that the student become the basis for organizing instruction rather than the teacher's predilections (based on training and past experience), that learning will be more productive when geared to data gathered at the grass roots level of the classroom than when imposed by official pronouncements filtering downward with consequent erosion.

In the following sections I shall try, first, to locate my notions of individualization in the context of other practices attempting to cope with individual differences and, second, to suggest a rather complex set of tasks that this approach suggests if indeed it is to have repercussions beyond that of a handy tool for isolated teachers.

Individualization

Patterns of Individualization

In previous allusions to the teacher's dilemma as he or she
observed gaps widening among students' achievements, it was
implied that any teacher worthy of the designation attempts to
cope with the problem and, indeed, a number of practices in the
past are characteristic of how schools have attempted to deal with
this concern.

Individual differences were recognized, for instance, by those
who, on the basis of the students' IQ, past academic performance,
or other measures, deemed it appropriate to exclude students
even from initial exposure to instruction. Others felt that
"flunking out" floundering students was a merciful procedure for
both the teacher and the learner. It is not my intent at this point
to discuss the merits or demerits of such elitist practices. They are
cited to illustrate the extreme position taken by those who, in the
name of lofty (sometimes arbitrary) absolute objectives, use
evidence often external to foreign-language study as a basis for
exclusion or inclusion. More recently, the advent of the FLES
movement has reopened the question of who should study foreign
languages. As might be expected, it was generally agreed that, in
a democratic system, all of the elementary school population was
entitled to be exposed to foreign-language instruction.[1] And yet,
the problem of uneven performance has served to keep alive such
measures as IQ, overall grades, and other academic factors as a
determinant to admission.[2]

Tracking represents a more comprehensive arrangement for
dealing with students of differing capabilities. The initial
assignment of students to the fast, middle, or slow groups, usually
on the basis of previous record, or the eventual placement of

students in respective ability groups on the basis of "performance" is predicated on teacher (or staff) estimate of their capability to cope with a global set of predetermined, absolute objectives. Such students are usually judged on the degree to which their achievements measure up to the overall, institutionally determined objectives of the "course." In such an arrangement, the objectives, often defined as the amount of material covered (vocabulary, grammar, etc.) remain constant. In spite of a school or department's philosophical stance and of its professed interest in adjusting the mechanics of instruction for pupils demonstrating different abilities, the syllabus (what is to be learned and at what rate of speed) is usually influenced by the achievement expected of the pupil on such external measures as College Boards, Regent's Examinations, Merit Scholar Competition, and so on.

A refinement of this procedure for dealing with "groups" of different abilities involves setting a common pace for all and providing, in the same class or across several classes, special opportunity for "enrichment" in the case of the gifted students and "remediation" for those unable to keep up with the preset goals.[3] Many instructors, sensitive to the widely divergent goals of "traditionalists" and "audio linguists," see the necessity of differentiating objectives for different groups of students. This is usually an either-or proposition. A given staff, in order to stimulate motivation, or simplify schedules, or reduce cost in money or energies, or simply avoid disaster and revolt, expediently decrees that a school is committed to a single objective. Sometimes, alternative programs are offered. But once a decision is taken it is irrevocable. No matter what insights are developed in subsequent exposure as to what the student really can do or what he really wants to achieve or what his response is to possible variations in the sequence of exposure and to integration of the various skills, the student is committed to this original decision.

As is often the case, selection is made on the oversimplified basis that, since passive skills are easier to acquire than active skills, less "gifted" students benefit most from a "reading" course. Just as regularly, a student expressing a vague desire to speak so he can "get along" if he goes abroad is committed to a "conversational" sequence that, as it eventually develops, may or may not be what he is best equipped to cope with.

A somewhat more sophisticated approach to individualization has to do with numbers, that is, the size of the group. In this approach the spectrum extends from the whole class working at the same task to one student working alone on a particular task. The intermittent possibilities provide for groups of 5 to 10 students operating as subgroups, all groups working at the same tasks or each groups working at a particular task. The composition of the respective groups may be varied: each group can be homogeneous, in which case each group is probably working at a different level of difficulty, or each group is heterogeneous, in which case all can operate at the same level of difficulty with the superior students in each group providing leadership in the group's activity, teaching the group, so to speak.[4]

A more subtle form of individualization takes place in a normal classroom when a sensitive teacher, well aware of each student's level of competence, directs student tasks (assignments, responses) in such a way that each student is required to perform only to the extent to which he is capable and in the area in which he is prepared. This approach, to the extent that it can be practiced, is probably the nearest to individualization manifest in the traditional classroom. An extension of this principle provides for individual work outside the group on the basis of a contract mutually agreed to by the student and the teacher.[5]

The above practices illustrate three basic ways in which individualization is usually conceptualized: (1) learners may be assigned different goals; (2) the same goals may be attained by the use of different approaches, methods, or techniques; (3) the same goals may be attained by the use of the same approaches, methods, or techniques but at different rates.[6]

I should like to suggest, that, as constructive as all or any of the above procedures may be, they need to be refined one step further.

I am not unaware of the demands that any form of individualization makes on teacher time. I am sensitive to the challenge that preparing teachers for a primary diagnostic function poses for teacher training. I contemplate seriously the amount of varied resources needed to provide appropriate tools for each student at specific points in the instructional sequence.

And yet, at the heart of the problem of individualization there is need to consider more seriously the determination of goals by students on the basis of aptitudes and attitudes. I am convinced that this is particularly crucial during the initial phase of instruction. For, in my estimation, the maximum situation of having one student working with one teacher (or cassette, or book, or whatever) speaks to individual activity rather than individualized learning unless the "input" is such that it fits the capacities and fills the needs of the one student involved in the activity. What is being restated here is that objectives must be selected and sequences determined on the basis of student reactions rather than on the basis of theoretical position or departmental policy.

Individualization and the Non-Student

The description of a beginning classroom in an earlier section was intentionally idealized. We were obviously describing a typical group of "good" students. Contrary to much of the current literature dealing with the monstrous problems allegedly characteristic of most classrooms, I feel that a good learning climate and reasonably responsive students tend to be the rule rather than the exception and that, in some measure at least, increasing the proportion of "good" classes, even in a traditional setting, is well within the province of the instructional staff. Without pretending that all is well in the better schools or that all schools contribute to quality education, I submit that the current trend has overgeneralized the punitive, futile directions of "traditional" education. There are, in my observation, a good number of schools in which learning is the rule, where students are relatively functional, and parents not totally distressed.[7]

It is assumed that, in such schools, a certain number of students will begin with a neutral "set" toward the various disciplines, including foreign languages. We cannot minimize the complex difficulties of dealing with groups of students who, corporately or individually, confront the school with a totally negative attitude. Very often this stance has deep roots in the social structure, and disruptive behavior in the classroom is only a manifestation of deep-rooted hostility. The student who considers the school as symbolic of a repressive system, who associates the role of the teacher with that of the oppressive law enforcer, who has convinced himself that all learning, if it is to be useful to him, must be counter to what the institution teaches, who has replaced the "myth" of education as a liberating influence with a myth of force or of lethargy as the only effective weapon available to juvenile cynicism—such a student presents a problem that is beyond the scope of the average teacher. We are thinking of the student alternating between hostility and apathy, suffering from cumulative academic deficit, lacking confidence, who compensates for his negative self-image through unrealistic aspirations completely irrelevant to the process of instruction.

The broad societal implications of this type of alienation call for dramatic measures, for a systematic restructuring of life experience as a prerequisite to reentry into the academic world. Such cases are clinical and deserve the full attention of the sociologist and psychologist, of specifically designed agencies with resources different from those available to the educational enterprise as currently structured.[8]

On the other hand, the school must often be held responsible for creating negative attitudes, causing students to shift from a positive set toward instruction. In general, the assumption that all students will be "ready" at the same time to react positively to a cast-iron curriculum structure, that each student must react with equal enthusiasm to any given subject, that the same formulation (more of the same is appropriate to the successful student as well as to the failing student)—this posture defies common sense and lacks basic humanity. And yet it prevails in many of our so-called educational institutions.

Furthermore, the student's attitude is often eroded by some usually dedicated teacher in more trivial but just as destructive ways. Still operating under the delusion that *magister dixit* is a viable formulation, the teacher-student relationship is too often characterized by teacher dominance with no attempt to communicate why the course is being taught, what the ground rules are, and what is to be the teacher's as well as the students' responsibility in converting the process into a tolerable educational experience. We need not belabor the fatal effect of punitive tests, unfocused activities, thoughtless assignments, and other well-meaning, irresponsible practices that serve to "turn students off."

The more sanguine "critics of the school" have long and loudly prescribed radical measures. These, summarily, amount to burning down the schools, decimating the existing instructional corps, and doing away with anything that remotely resembles subject matter.[9] Although I am sympathetic to the critics' concerns, I consider their solution nihilistic and counter-productive. More effort needs to be directed to effecting transition between the imperfect and the visionary and less to verbal castigations often grounded in overgeneralized observations and cathartic, sentimental confessions. I fully endorse aspirations toward a noble goal but am convinced that faith without works is dead and that evolution rather than revolution will be more productive in the long run.

In this context, the concept of individualization is instrumental in improving educational practices. Recognizing the student's needs, interest, and capabilities is important to a more flexible approach to curriculum. Student reaction becomes central in determining the subjects to which the students are exposed, the time at which exposure begins, and the duration of the exposure, depending on individual reaction to the initial phase. I am not suggesting that valuing student reactions means abrogating teacher responsibilities. I sympathize with the teacher in whom role conflict has become an obsession, particularly if his subject (foreign languages among others) does not obviously "grab" the majority of his students. He has no alternative, at the professional level, but to seek other modes of employment.[10] In short, while I endorse the removal of the existing system of requirements as inevitable, I see this as altogether different from removing the subject from the school offering as an elective appropriate at different times to satisfy the curiosity or to meet the aspirations of a given number of students.[11]

This has serious implications for the future of foreign-language studies. For, if choice of subject is, by and large, a student decision, then each subject becomes competitive with all others. And it is apparent that the study of a foreign language, usually undertaken with vague long-range objectives, characterized by a long sequence of instruction, punctuated by tedium and discouragement, does not stand up well in the educational showcase. It cannot compete with the three R's on the basis of utility or with the social sciences on the basis of social relevance or with the arts on the basis of joy-giving self-expression.

In spite of these apparent liabilities, I submit that, in the present as in the past, a reasonable proportion of students, out of curiosity, or because they assert a professional or intellectual or aesthetic need, will explore the area of foreign languages. The prospects for the future depend on the degree to which we can move those students beginning foreign-language study with at least a neutral set toward eventual endorsement of their experience as productive, enjoyable, and, most important, successful in terms of individual aspirations. Therein lies the challenge to which there is no facile alternative. Therein lies the call to action for concerted professional effort.[12]

7   Priorities

Articulation

In previous passages, I tried to outline a working system through which individual teachers, by focusing on a discrete corpus of material from different perspectives, could attempt to individualize instruction. Let us now address ourselves to establishing a parameter common for all introductory courses, which will tend to give a common shape to the diversity of activities suggested by the modular approach.

The need for defining such a parameter is evident as we survey and summarize the long and usually distressing documentation relevant to the problem identified as "articulation." For many, failure to "articulate" has been considered a major deterrent in maintaining student interest in foreign-language instruction. Anecdotal reports describe the plight of the student who moves from his elementary class to a high school and realizes that he is ill-prepared, that he has learned nothing of accepted value in the high-school sequence, and that his only alternative is to start over again.[1] Just as numerous, though less emotionally loaded, are the cases where the successful high-school student emerges "unqualified" to place beyond the elementary college course or to cope with the content of foreign-language requirements as structured in higher education.[2]

Lack of articulation can be attributed to a number of causes. Disagreement as to general course objectives is bound to arise, depending on the level of instruction: "developing positive attitudes" may be appropriate in the early grades; "ability to communicate in a social situation" may characterize the goals of the high-school course; "reading documents essential to research activities" is plainly justified at the graduate level. There is little evidence that serious attempts were made in the past to see each objective as appropriate to a given point in the continuum of a long sequence. Instead, each segment of the instructional corps has tended to deprecate the achievements at other levels, to view alternative goals as mutually exclusive.

The condition is further acerbated because students in different age groups respond to different teaching strategies and react positively to different materials of instruction. The topical interest of the materials, the sophistication of the "intellectual" content, the amount of available time for mastering a given unit must be taken into account as one moves from one level of instruction to the next. If, in spite of these variables, achievement is measured at a given point by instruments reflecting a particular (sometimes peculiar) position, the student being tested will be evaluated for what he cannot possibly know rather than for what he does know.

Most of this discussion has focused on the foreign-language sequence prior to college instruction. There is no intent to disregard college efforts or minimize college problems. However, the college situation, to date at least, has been "special" in that colleges are dealing with a population that has been selected for its general academic achievement and motivation and that has furthermore been narrowed down by self-selection as to subject concentration. It therefore seems futile to argue against literature-oriented sequences designed, generally, to meet the needs of those students prepared for and intent on moving in that direction. We are less concerned with redefining college goals than with suggesting that they might be broadened to include other intellectual and career options appropriate to foreign-language study. Articulation of the foreign-language sequence from high school to college is considered not only as a means of accommodating students but as a symptom of the degree of professional solidarity, of mutual responsibility. At a more pedestrian level, there is evidence that many colleges have not given sufficient attention and support to earlier instruction as the pipeline that, in the long run, supplies colleges and justifies their existence.[3]

Unwillingness to communicate, inflexibility, callous disregard for student sensitivities have been advanced as obstacles to bridging the gaps between the grades, high school, and the college campus. Unfortunately, these symptoms are often discernible within a single system, even within a single grade. The individual teacher's inability or unwillingness to be "pinned down" by specified objectives, inconsistencies between stated goals and classroom practices, idiosyncratic and arbitrary modes of evaluation, defensiveness, insularity, and professional jealousies have often resulted in a variety of highly colorful and individualistic sequences that, unfortunately, have penalized the student when he moves from one class to another or from one grade to the next.

To say that, in the past, the situation has been acerbated by commitment to the "traditional" as opposed to the "audio-lingual" approach is an oversimplification. There is evidence, however, that methodological slogans, at least in part, did serve to justify inflexibility in both camps.

Commonality Wanted

Polarization toward the "New Key" as opposed to the "traditional" approach has tended to obfuscate human factors significant to the survival of foreign-language instruction. As a result, foreign-language teachers were bombarded with prescriptions that, in many cases, not only sanctified the one true way to salvation but that, conversely, castigated as flagrant heresy any departure from the hallowed doctrine. Priorities called for emphasizing hearing and speaking as the prime objectives of instruction, for insisting on second-language learning as aiming at "compound" bilingualism, for mastering structures through induction, and so forth. But, by the same token, the reading-writing skills were often deprecated as threatening the purity of the doctrine, "grammar" became associated with the smell of brimstone, and such practices as translation, presenting vocabulary out of context, introducing culture as extraneous to language, occasional use of English in class, and speaking at less than frenzied speed were considered by the more extreme as paving the road to perdition.

Inversely, exponents of the "old way" backlashed with Olympian contempt, with total condemnation (usually unsupported even by personal experience) of a system that turned students into parrots through dialogue memorization, that reduced them to imbecility by protecting them from the rigors of grammatical analysis, that dehumanized them in the impersonal and isolated conditions provided by the laboratory.

Even under optimum conditions, in situations when intra- and interlevel communication occurred, where a consensus to broad objectives and common methodologies prevailed, poor articulation still militated against the struggling student. For, often, the lack of concordance between the lexical and structural loading of various texts or other core materials of instruction made transfer from one sequence to another nearly the equivalent of starting another language.

I cite my own experience as we moved students from a "modern" first-year text to a more traditional second-year text, both published by the same company. Suspecting discrepancies in vocabulary loading, I initiated a tabulation that would enable us to gradually introduce the discrepant words as a necessary step in moving into the second-year book. The magnitude of the task was astounding, beyond the wildest apprehension. To affect a reasonably smooth transition we were faced with the task of making up roughly 1,200 words, which had been part of the sequence in one first-year course and to which the students had not been exposed in the first-year book they used in the previous year.

Again, a rough survey of the vocabulary loading of two major first-year audio-lingual texts shows that coincidence rather than intent is probably the explanation for such concomitance as occurs:

	Total Loading	Common Items 1st Quarter	Common Items 2nd Quarter	Common Items 3rd Quarter	Total Common Items
Text X	905				
		259	34	17	310
Text Y	670				

Without belaboring the point, it is evident that, as far as vocabulary is concerned, even a "successful" student having completed Text X is able to cope with only one-half of the material covered in Text Y and that a comparable student initiated through Text Y can be expected to deal with only a third of the material covered in Text X.

The discrepancies are even more serious if we consider that the overlap occurs principally in the first quarter and that a fair percentage of the common stock is made up of high-frequency function words. It is obvious that the longer the course progresses the slighter the possibility of equitably transferring students from one system to another.

The problem of commonality of structures seems less acute because, when initiated in dialogue in the early stages of instruction, they may be treated more like vocabulary to be learned by rote than like structures. It is interesting to note that they are finally selected as models for structural analysis in a sequence reminiscent of the organization of traditional grammars.

The profession has increasingly become concerned with "levels" of performance and that has certainly been a move in the right direction. According to this concept the student is "placed" according to his demonstrated ability to perform a number of predetermined objectives rather than on the basis of time of exposure. A valiant effort has been made to reach consensus on general objectives. A characteristic Level I objective is to "Comprehend the language spoken at normal classroom speed, within the range of vocabulary and constructions found in the more generally used Level I textbooks."[4] If our analysis of lexical discrepancies between textbooks is even partially correct, the above objective becomes meaningless in assessing achievement or facilitating articulation.

The above observations lead us to make a desperate plea for concerted professional effort to reach consensus on the lexical and structural parameters for at least the first two levels of foreign-language instruction as the first condition of improved articulation. Granted the constraints implied in such a decision, we see it as essential to justice in the classroom for purposes of instruction and evaluation.

The task is certainly feasible since frequency lists based on the conversational skills are available in many foreign languages.[5] Granted the ambiguities attending frequency lists, the ones available can certainly provide a solid base for further refinements.[6] A more functional list will eventually emerge, which, while taking into consideration pedagogical concerns, will also reflect the student's need to communicate outside as well as in the classroom on topics congenial to his interest. Given the availability (and imperfections) of frequency lists, we are still in need of a systematic study of school talk for various age levels. A research project involving the recording of students as they chat in the hall, in the locker room, or in "bull sessions" would provide a base for the kind of lexical repertoire that students need if they are to indulge in free, meaningful communication. In short, development of improved common lexical and structural parameters is a task calling for the cooperation of teacher, student, and researcher.

The proposition raises the specter of regimentation. The problem is not whether the parameters can be determined and agreed upon in theory but whether or not the teaching corps will accept them in practice. We must give it a try on the general supposition that the more precise the parameter the greater the latitude provided for individual creativity within the stable parameter. It may be that teachers, up to now straining under the yoke of imposed methodology, may welcome an opportunity to individualize their style while still assured that common content ensures the achievement of common professional goals.

8 Contributions Welcome

Linguistics

The previous section has treated desiderata that, to a large degree, depended on teacher participation and teacher control. Let us now turn to other resources, which, because they are technical, are beyond the purview of the typical practitioner.

Without suggesting that linguistics should redefine its goals and modes of operation, we propose that, from the perspective of classroom instruction, there is need to broaden the scope of operation by at least a portion of those qualified as linguists or applied linguists.

First, there is need for continued emphasis on translating scientific language into terms that are comprehensible to the teacher as an interpreter and implementer of new and old doctrines.[1] Explications of the shift from the structural to the transformational generative approach suggests that this can be achieved with at least some measure of success. The merits and limitations of teaching major "patterns" (surface grammar) so that a given stimulus will elicit a correct automatic response and subsequently lead to generalizations instrumental in formulating subsequent analogies have been thoroughly discussed in relation to second-language performance. More recently, a good case is being made to attempt to exploit more significantly the learner's language competence, his innate grasp of deep structures that permit him to perform language functions in a more creative vein. Any interested language teacher presently has available articles that illuminate the respective theories and point up positive as well as negative implications for classroom practices.[2]

Hope for the future depends on new creative concepts, on the development and refinement of linguistic theories. The practioner, to the extent possible, must remain informed of new insights and become increasingly sensitive to the implications of recent theories as translated by dedicated mediators. It is important, however, that professionals resist the temptation to climb aboard the latest bandwagon, especially if it implies rejecting those contributions that have had significant impact on teaching. It cannot be forgotten that by training and experience the teacher's expertise focuses on problems of performance and that he may not yet be ready to explore the teaching of competence, a still illusive area in first-language learning.

As noted in several sections of this essay, there is now available to the teacher a substantial literature on phonemics and on contrastive analysis of the structure of English and many other languages.[3] This has been translated into a number of effective practices, a variety of models for structural drills that, it is hoped, will continue to be valued in the teacher's arsenal of instructional techniques.[4]

Meanwhile, the teacher is in a position to call the theorist's attention to a number of areas that have been neglected. To date, the emphasis (by definition) has focused on the verbal aspects of language. If there is any merit to a multiskill approach in the initial phase of instruction, the teacher will need an additional set of directions provided by experts in the science of language to facilitate his task.

A number of instructional problems call for additional theoretical underpinnings as a prerequisite to the design and dissemination of easily accessible materials, mini-units if you will, intended to individualize learning and produce better performance in a number of skills and subskills. It is my contention that, at present, progress is assumed to occur in a nebulous way. We still tend to equate exposure with internalization. It is my conviction that better results are obtained when each objective is taught in a systematic way. Exercises are needed to reinforce process at the minimal as well as global level.

Resources are insufficient even in the aural-oral area. For

instance, while phonetic contrasts have been described there has been little attention paid to developing the capacity to discriminate at various speeds of delivery. Few systematic exercises are available for developing in the student his ability to differentiate, in the total utterance, word boundaries, stem from ending, the significance of one ending as opposed to another, to isolate in a systematic way the central component from the secondary, elaborative aspects as they are integrated in the original message. In the past emphasis on "understanding" the total communication, too little attention has been paid to becoming conscious of the components as part of a repertoire for generating additional messages. Another area completely neglected concerns understanding familiar speech. Although the differences between formal and informal delivery have often been discussed with respect to cultural implication or relative merit, no set of exercises has been devised to facilitate the transition, for instance, from "school French" (/ilniakǝnu; uɛsǝkǝtyva/) to "street French" (/jaknu; uktyva/). This area also has implications for pronunciation and spelling.

At the speaking level much attention has been paid to the description of various phonemes with little attention to the production of those through approximation or through maximizing the development of what essentially constitutes the control of involuntary muscles.[5] Little attention has been paid to the problem of syllabication as contributing to the proper sequencing of polysyllabic words. While much attention has been given to stress and intonation, few drills are available for assuring delivery in proper breath groups, for emphasizing the necessity of flow without the mastery of which two subskills, stress and intonation, remain isolated and unrelated to overall communication.

These deficiencies are compounded if one believes that accurate oral reading is important, at least for some people, as preliminary to use of the written text. Since the artificial device of learning through the phonetic alphabet was discarded (with some justification) little (except delaying exposure to the printed word) has been put at the service of teachers and students to ensure reading aloud correctly. A complete "package" might well be devised to cope with problems of graphemic-phonemic correspondence, silent final letters, diacritical signs, punctuation, anomalies, and the special interference created by recognizable cognates. At a more sophisticated level the techniques and hardware available to the reading specialist might well be adapted to second-language reading to ensure proper eye movement and consequent acceptable "flow." I am proposing a systematic study of techniques available to second-language reading development. As examples a number of devices (AVR Eye-Span Trainer, Cenco Overhead Projection Reading Pacer) might contribute to improving oral reading habits and other audiovisual techniques for controlling speed and accuracy of visual-conceptual association might well be adopted for the foreign-language diagnostic and learning center.[6]

In context reading, which is important in its own right and also as a tool made available to individual instruction and to evaluation, first of all we need to go back to what we already know about teaching this particular skill before it was adumbrated by emphasis on the conversational skills.[7]

Even more important, the two subskills need to be carefully analyzed in relation to each other to determine the extent to which, usually unconsciously, the student is unable to decode because of difficulty with correct voicing or reads aloud badly as a result of being distracted because he does not know the meaning of a word or does not recognize the relationship of various components of the message to each other.

The revered "dictée" often reflects our casual approach to instruction. While this venerable transplant is, by and large, a legitimate spelling test in its natural environment it tends to be punitive in the foreign-language class setting unless carefully limited to the lexical, structural, and conceptual repertoire of the students. Even when carefully controlled, it is often given before sufficient systematic instruction in spelling has been provided the student. Deprived of sufficient practice in transcribing sounds according to the arcane canons of foreign orthography, the student is left no alternative but approximations, wild inferences, and many blanks on the page.[8]

The situation calls for systematic, corrective drills on sound-letter(s) correspondence, diacritical signs, anomalies, punctuation, and so on, as a prerequisite to eventually dealing with the mystifying effects of sometimes bizarre morphological "rules."

"Free" composition, since it involves recall as well as application, is even more complicated than dictation. It therefore calls for incremental development of a repertoire of lexical and structural items before students are put in a hopeless situation in which they have, as alternatives, either meaningless exteriorization or fits of frustration and despair.

It is realized that, in each of these areas, drills cannot be provided to cover the infinite number of contingencies inherent in communication. It is suggested, however, that sufficient exercises for each skill and subskill are available to provide teachers and students with at least minimal models for proceeding in a less than haphazard way, for supplying an appropriate tool that can at least serve to initiate correctly what is acknowledged as a long and continuous process.

While recommendations for improved instrumentation in each category do not suggest an insurmountable task, I should like to suggest the initiation of studies focusing on facilitating the "transfer" of accepted performance in one skill to another skill. For, if individualization implies, at least in part, mastery of a language component regardless of the sequence of the skills through which it is attacked, we need to identify and develop instructional tools by which this transfer can be maximized. The thrust in the last few years has given some insights into a process that involves speech as a base for eventual exposure to reading and writing. More attention must now be paid to the visual-minded (the student who can spell a word once he has seen it) and to the more analytically inclined (the student who insists on grasping a generalization before he will emit a single utterance). For individuals in these categories also deserve the opportunity to succeed, each according to his particular gift.

Psychology

As has already been noted in the previous overview of linguistics,

the transformation of theories of psychology into effective
instructional practices is a complicated task that often leaves the
practitioner more bewildered than encouraged. At the psycholinguistic level investigations are not yet conclusive as to the
complexities attending first-language learning and the distinctions to be made between first and second language. Nor are we
clear as to the effects that knowing a first language have on the
process of learning a second one in terms of chronological age and
linguistic sophistication. We do not have sufficiently specific
formulation as to how to exploit the linguistic baggage obviously
acquired in first-language learning to make second language
more effective.[9]

The teacher is therefore in the ambiguous position of wanting
and needing to know more while being warned that he cannot rely
too heavily on psychology or linguistics since these fields are not
yet ready to provide the synthesis that would illuminate the
teacher's task.[10] Yet the teacher is aware of a number of salient
problems that he observes day after day. Although he often is
unable to ascribe them to a particular field of experimental
psychology and cannot describe them in technical terms, he is
convinced intuitively that they have to do with perception,
cognition, motivation that he perceives as the domain of
psychology.

He is puzzled by blocks to memorizing and despairs when he
considers how quickly much that is learned is forgotten. He is
often uncomprehending as to why obviously bright students show
little perseverance as they confront the foreign-language learning
task. He keeps asking himself why, since all students have
demonstrated "intelligence" to communicate in one language, a
great number demonstrate almost complete incompetence when
challenged with a second language. He suspects that there is
something "radically wrong" in the basic instrumentation of the
foreign-language class, something fundamental that he cannot
hope to remedy without help from experts and specialists.

Then, there is a different order of questions that he can at least
formulate. Many of these lead him to informal, random
experimentation in the classroom that sometimes succeeds and
sometimes fails. A few typical questions follow.

Given a new student with a neutral attitude, how might the teacher learn more about those nonlinguistic aspects of instructional circumstances that might increase his interest? Does a properly decorated classroom really make a difference? What is truly the effect of putting the student in contact with foreigners? It is assumed that the answer to these questions is a resounding "Yes," and yet, in my observations, the institution of such practices often prove disappointing in terms of measurable effect.

The recent trend has pointed to increasing emphasis on current events, to the use of periodicals, and so on. And yet we know very little about what type of current events or what subjects in the periodicals (music, politics, sex) are of general interest to all students or of particular interest to students of different sex, age groups, academic orientation, socioeconomic condition. We still need to question what portions of the foreign culture (presented visually or through an English text) "turn him on" and what topics are stimulating to students of various age levels.

Although any good school has foreign-language clubs, these usually focus on a single language and end up providing a distraction for "exceptional" students. A more potent single-language club would involve all languages (including English) and would provide a forum for serious discussion of language qua language, for an interdisciplinary approach to culture. Such a setting might well serve to determine the importance of student interaction on the topic of foreign languages among students of the same language, among students of different languages, between language students and those having opted out of foreign-language study. In short, we need more documentation concerning the impact of various practices on different types of students. To what extent are all the above more important for instrumental than for integrative students? If a student enters the foreign-language class merely "curious," in what way do we sustain and whet his curiosity?

There is, in effect, a consensus that consistent failure will eventually discourage students, reduce their drive and their persistence, and will finally produce total apathy or hostility. If success is the opposite of failure, it will produce opposite results: interest, persistence, encouragement. Yet we have no specific formulation on the amount and kind of success that will result in predictable behavior for different types of learners at different levels. Are good grades a mark of success for some, while for others success means only reaching a plateau from which to respond to the challenge of a more stimulating task? Is success the same for the equilibrium-seeking as for the tension-responsive individual? Is it an intrinsic reward for some and extrinsic for others? Are there personal differences in the degree of response of immediate as opposed to long-range gratification?

Once success has been defined, in what way can the skill-learning task be structured to ensure a measure of success for all? For whom is a single-skill approach superior to a multiskill approach? There is some evidence that one category of students achieves equally well in all language skills, that another category continues to achieve well in at least one skill but resists exposure to the others, and that a third category remains unresponsive to interventions designed to develop sustained interest in even one of the skills.[11]

It is pertinent to ask also: What teaching strategy is more congenial to one than to another student?[12] What are the various ways that memorization and retention best can be stimulated? How do individuals respond to various types of mnemonic aids?[13] What organization of materials, sequencing of skills, and use of supportive activities is most appropriate for different types of students? Which students need to be carefully nurtured in the area of self-determination and which seem to be "ready" at the onset to order their own learning? For teachers must be particularly sensitive to this problem if they are to move from a traditional classroom structure. One of the principal pitfalls attending individualization is constituted by the notion that all students are capable of handling the responsibility of "directing their own learning." Faced with this challenge, many students respond energetically, others cry a lot, and many others simply "goof off." It is generally agreed that chronological age, temperament, previous life-style, and the overall climate of the school are all significant factors influencing the individual's capacity for self-direction. The degree of responsibility to be assumed, the character of the task to be attacked, and the availability of resources that the student can handle are complicating factors. The latter has particular significance to foreign-language studies since, particularly in the early stages, the student is inevitably dependent on models, inexperienced in how to locate resources, and incapable of applying appropriate criteria to estimate the degree to which his efforts are moving him in the right direction.

There is no particular merit to a long list of queries, and yet clarifying the numerous questions outlined above may be vital in increasing the effectiveness of foreign-language learning. Answers to any or all of them are of crucial importance to the development of new materials, to the planning of more productive activities, and to the designing of powerful interventions. In the long run, in addition to working toward generalizations and synthesis, the task to which psychology has much to contribute involves determining what a specific child can learn best, how best he achieves his limited goal as a prerequisite to eventually expanding his objectives to more complex and complete aspirations.

Technology

As indicated in a previous section, I see the usefulness of any "machine" as directly correlated to the availability of materials appropriate to the function of the apparatus and to the extent it contributes to reaching one or several instructional objectives.

The purpose of this section is to indicate several ways in which existing equipment needs to be improved or adapted to foreign-language instruction and to explore new directions in which technology might turn its attention, particularly with a view to contributing to more individualized instruction.

Such standard equipment as record players and tape recorders must have provision for instant stop and restart. Ideally, provisions should be made for controlling the speed of the sound track and consequently the speed of speech delivery without producing extreme changes in pitch and timbre. Random access control is also an advantage. Sound and filmstrip projectors are needed that increase simplicity of operation by providing, in a single compact unit, manual and remote control, rear-view projection, and automatic synchronization of picture and sound. The capacity to select appropriate frames is also needed.

Motion picture projectors (both 16-mm. and 8-mm.), to be most useful, must feature cartridge loading, stop motion, and reverse.

Teaching machines ranging from manually operated "response cards" (under $30) to models providing synchronized audiovisual presentation ($400-$1,000) are available and suggest a multitude of applications to the teaching of various foreign-language skills and subskills. As an example, several models of "talking card readers" are available. These compact devices are useful for individual work, provide listen-record-compare features and simultaneous exposure to sound and visual stimuli, both pictorial and graphic.[14]

With a resurgent interest in reading skill there are possibilities in the use of equipment and techniques effective in teaching English. The profession, preferably working with reading specialists, might well consider using equipment currently available for improving recognition of letter and letter combinations, for developing proper pace in oral reading, for improving comprehension and reading speed. Ideally, in the case of foreign language, synchronization of graphic symbols with sounds is indicated.[15]

While programmed instruction holds great promise for several aspects of foreign-language instruction, to date it has had little effect on the teaching of foreign languages. Carroll's comments in 1968 seem appropriate.

. . . . We now have better information about the role of motivation in language study, but no better ways of increasing that motivation. Programmed instruction in foreign languages is still in its infancy because of the grave technological and economic problems involved in audio-visual programmed instruction. Computer-based instruction seems feasible, but will be very expensive.[16]

Determination to incorporate the computer in foreign-language instruction may prove a catalyst to programming. A major constraint limiting this thrust resides in the fact that self-

monitoring in terms of speech production, important to the
elementary level, is still a challenge unmet by technology. Even
such ambitious programs as PLATO illustrate the wide gap and
the time lag separating promising prototypes and institutional
availability of computerized programs.[17]

To this point we have discussed features involving equipment
now directly available to the teacher in the classroom or that
might become available without prohibitive cost. Other
possibilities hold promise but involve major installations and/or a
concerted thrust at the organizational level.

It would be hoped that the success of Sesame Street would
stimulate the foreign-language profession to renew its interest in
educational television. We see possibilities in recording attractive
mini-units, not oriented to presenting part of a "course" through
a teacher cast in the role of "star" but rather an attempt to bring
all techniques to bear on illustrative visuals focusing on a single
step in the accretion of a particular skill.[18]

Videotape, with a successful record as an effective training
device in teacher preparation, may be a useful instrument in
fostering motivation in the classroom and providing teacher and
student with a common basis for observation, comparison, and
discussion. One of the main assets of video taping is that the
machine provides its own audiovisual software.[19]

Basically, the claim of technology that the equipment is either
available, on the drawing board, or can be invented is probably
valid. If technology is to serve foreign-language instruction to the
maximum, it is incumbent on teachers to specify in terms of their
own needs what is required for a specific task and, on the basis of
their judgment and experience, to dictate to manufacturers what
serves their purpose best. Commercial houses, at this time, feel
insufficient pressure to improve their wares and have too few
professional resources to turn to for advice.

In view of the loosening of prescriptions of what is the
"proper" sequence for teaching the several language skills as
well as increasing speculations of the viability of a multiskill,
multisensory approach, the development of appropriate
equipment and materials seems imperative and must be inspired
and monitored by professional expertise.

Insofar as ideal equipment is often expensive or that use of technology implies a learning systems approach, the school might well reconsider the administrative aspects of the problem and begin to think in terms of consortia, of equipment centers available to the community as well as to a single building.

The pattern has already been set by the business sector, offering, in direct competition to the schools, to produce concrete results in terms of specific, realistic objectives. Within admitted limitations, individualized audiovisual programmed instruction may soon be contracted out of the purview of the school.[20]

9   New Directions

Culture

A previous section discussed efforts to make culture integral to the foreign-language sequence and how these efforts are still besieged by dilemmas and paradoxes.

One of the most important obstacles, that of dealing with culture exclusively through the foreign language, is one that to date has been treated with appalling ambiguity with the result that exposure to significant cultural phenomena has been seriously limited. This can be attributed in part at least to the doctrinaire position of extremists who insist on exclusive use of the foreign language in all phases of instruction. At worst, it has led to the indefinite deferment of serious discourse about culture. At best, it has resulted in a distorted view of culture acquired only after painful and frustrating confrontation with language problems. The student, eager to wrestle with significant social and political issues, is denied opportunity to deal with these with the complete resources of his conceptual and native language repertoire. The frustrations he experiences are just as real as those produced by premature exposure to literature but the reasons are inverted. In each case he is reduced to imbecility (imposed in one case and real in another) while asked to deal with higher order intellectual problems.[1]

If there is any merit (and I believe there is) in breaking down monocultural myopia, if, indeed, this is considered a serious task, I propose that it be treated in a serious manner.

Before and during the prolonged labors involved in developing language skills students should be exposed in English to cultural materials that are appropriate to their interest and level of maturity.

Furthermore, I submit that a direct effort in this direction is essential as part of the general curriculum whether or not the child is enrolled in a foreign-language class. A class offered under the auspices of an interdisciplinary committee will be responsible for addressing itself to cultural differences and similarities observable among the many nations of the world. It may well be that such a course might involve members of the foreign-language staff who, through expertise and personal experience, are in a position to make significant contributions in interpreting attitudes, values, and mores of the country whose language and culture is familiar to them.

This argument poses a threat to entrenchment and catalyzes parochial jealousies. But I see no alternative and even consider the possibility of great benefits to the foreign-language cause. For, assuming the removal of "requirement" and the effect of capricious trends, there is the need, in the immediate future, to provide new sources of stimulation that will promote students' enrolling in the foreign-language sequence. Exposure to culture seen as a legitimate goal in itself, in many cases, will serve to arouse curiosity toward a certain country. This, in turn, will serve as a solid rationale for entering the skill-development phase of the appropriate language with better than neutral attitudes.

It would seem that, even in the initial stage, the interest of students engaged in foreign-language study might be sustained by continued collateral readings, discussion in English along lines predicated by interest in crucial historical and contemporary problems. The traditional unit on explorers (fifth or sixth grade), which often marks the high point in articulating content with foreign language, is a case in point. Though still in the rudimentary phase of foreign-language development, the student is able to cope only with superficial aspects of the problem (names, geography, country of origin) whereas he is still already able to intellectualize around such topics as colonization, economic and political prestige, international jealousies, and the logistics of war and peace. The real tragedy is that this condition will continue to deteriorate for a long time before, eventually, if ever, it gets better. The student continues to mature at a constant, rapid rate while his language skills, on the basis of a very limited exposure, inch slowly upward. The gap between his desire to communicate and his ability to communicate increases in proportion to the time of exposure.

There is even the possibility of making culture more relevant in at least two directions. By forsaking the past Mecca syndrome (focus on the alleged source of culture: Paris, Rome, Madrid, etc.), the student's vision is expanded to think in global, international rather than in prescriptive, parochial terms. Dealing with all francophone countries, for example, opens up the cultural "trip" to include Canada. The proximity of Canada makes field trips relatively inexpensive. The students come to grips with a bilingual situation in which juxaposition of two languages is evident in street signs, advertising, and published documents.[2]

Interest in Swahili and other African tongues is an expression of the black community's interest in establishing links with Africa.[3] A case can be made for the teaching of languages as a productive, academic experience for the "disadvantaged."[4] More importantly, since French is the official language of many African countries, black Americans have interest in mastering that language as a key to political and economic participation and as a means of becoming sensitive interpreters of negritude, the significant theme inspiring much of the excellent literature indigenous to francophone countries in which blacks are called to play a dominant political and intellectual role as they bridge the gap between colonization and independent, emerging nations.

Teachers of Spanish have a better record of including the culture of Spanish-speaking countries in the Americas as part of the total cultural fabric. And yet, attention has but recently turned to the cultural and language problems of a sizable portion of our own population. That is not to say that interest in problems of language maintenance and in the deprivation of Spanish-speaking Americans is new. The March 1965 issue of *Modern Language Journal* is a symposium dealing with bilingualism and the bilingual child (vol. 49, no. 3). The March and April issues (vol. 3, nos. 3, 4) provide additional insights into the complexities of the situation. But the recent shift from awareness of the problem to well-supported action programs intended to solve it is yet another example of the capriciousness of the national conscience *vis à vis* ethnic groups and the important role of language in societal determination. Academic interest is seldom translated into social action without pressure. The civil rights movement is an unexpected agency for highlighting Spanish-speaking Americans whose culture contributes to our national pluralism, whose language competence constitutes a wasted resource, and whose plight speaks to the insensitivity of the national conscience.

Given our capacity to overlook the obvious, it is not surprising that, in the case of the more exotic languages, the surface of existing possibilities has hardly been scratched. As an illustration, we see the move to transplant Hebrew from the religious into the community school as a by-product of international developments rather than as part of a long-range national plan. As a nation we respond well to crisis situations (Sputnik: Russian) but seem predictably improvident in anticipating the crisis itself (Chinese, Japanese, etc.).

A second emphasis that might make the cultural dialogue more relevant and more productive from the point of view of international interaction leads to a consideration not only of foreign influences on the United States but equal consideration of the effect of American culture (whether considered good or bad) on the traditions, behavior, and aspirations of other nations that, directly or indirectly, have been exposed to the alleged naïveté and brutality of the American dream, who may or may not agree with the democratic ideal, but who, nevertheless, have not been left untouched by concepts of relative popular opulence, mechanization, technology, and organizational effectiveness.

In a different vein, it seems that, in recent generations, language has been neglected as a source of inquiry dealing with significant human behavior. In recent years, synchronic rather than diachronic analyses have been seen as more relevant to language-teaching activities partially on the basis that more scientific rigor is possible in the case of the former. While this has been a move in the right direction, it has occurred at the expense of historical linguistics that, because it often depends on inference rather than observation, allows for a maximum of speculation and adds an element of romance to the element of precision. It may be suggested that, in addition to cultural distinctions emerging from the content of the skill-development materials, much could be done by reviving philological interest (within or beyond the context of class materials).

Selected examples suffice to instill in those students interested (and in my experience they are not in the minority) the fragile, complex, persistent, dynamic evolution of language as illustrative of human caprice and creativity.

The evolution of structural features of language, in a single language or in contrast to other languages, has fascination for some. Changes due to semantic shifts, to folk etymology, and to borrowings, as well as the historical factors influencing stability or precipitating change, are in a given language important cultural milestones well worth the attention of an inquiring mind. At a rudimentary level, the cultural significance of a foreign language can be easily exploited locally through analysis of proper names, street names, and so forth. Place names in general are particularly instructive in considering language mutations and the cultural and historical forces that have left them as our legacy.[5]

Last, the thrust toward establishing cultural contrasts as a prerequisite to mediating differences has generally led to neglect of universal consonance. In trying to establish national cultural differences too few distinctions have been made among ethnic, social, and economic differences. Too little attention has been paid to those common traits binding the human family, particularly in the relationship of Western European countries to the United States. Beauty, whimsy, joyfulness, intuitive or rational concern for cosmic problems permeating human destinies have not sufficiently been exploited as a means of relating people to people as they grope their way through the seven ages of man.

I am not suggesting indiscriminate, extensive readings in translation as a substitute for enjoying the original text. Great books in any language must be read in the original to appreciate style, but what essentially makes them great is the universal appeal of the content.

Innovations

If innovation denotes departure from past concepts and practices, our entire discussion of the audio-lingual movement including philosophy, classroom practices, and utilization of new media has spoken to significant innovations that characterized foreign-language teaching in the last two decades. A number of more recent concepts having increasing impact on instruction seems, for our purpose, integral to the general heading of curriculum. These will be discussed in a subsequent section. Discussion here will be limited to three areas that seem to have direct implications for individualized instruction.[6]

Although team teaching, modular scheduling, and staff differentiation each represents a different emphasis and entered the educational limelight in chronological order, for purposes of economy all three will be considered in relationship to one another rather than each as an entity.

All three concepts represent attempts to individualize teaching, a departure from the notion of the teacher as an inter-changeable part assigned to an arbitrary section of the master-schedule without concern for his or her predications or capacities.

Team teaching emphasizes staff intercommunication, the result being more judicious use of teacher specialization in both the planning and implementation of the scheduled, pre-determined time slots. Implicit in the arrangement is the possibility of modifying group sizes on the basis of appropriate-ness to a given activity and of supporting teacher activities by means of paraprofessionals and mechanical aids. The elementary and middle schools have provided a logical setting for this type of arrangement since self-contained classrooms provided more inherent flexibility than the high school committed to the scheduling rigidities implied in cutting across several subject-matter boundaries.[7]

Modular scheduling, on the contrary, is a primary mechanical device intended to focus on the time distribution most appropriate to various academic (subject-matter) activities. In principle, and contrary to the "traditional" distribution of time, certain subjects because of the nature of the subject and the activities indicated in the teaching thereof can best be taught in large blocks of time (bi- or tri-weekly), while others can best be assimilated through frequent exposure on a daily basis or even twice a day. The mechanics or modular scheduling are intended to provide opportunity for groups of different sizes to be exposed to different instructional inputs as determined by staff judgment.[8]

While differentiated staffing presupposes ideal conditions as far as distribution of available time and relies heavily on inter-communication as determining the matrix in which individual contributions can best be organized, it emphasizes more formally the specialization feature mentioned above. Any given "team" is hierarchized in terms of qualification, predilections, function, and financial rewards. Performance in terms of contributions to the total project is the essential criterion rather than level of formal education, seniority, or other considerations.[9]

These innovative practices, as attractive as they seem to be (singly or in combination) to anyone disenchanted with the "egg crate" school, have been better described than evaluated. By and large the advances they promise have only been realized on a limited basis or, in many cases, been corrupted or diluted beyond recognition. This may speak more eloquently to the teacher's penchant for the traditional than to inherent weaknesses in the concepts.

These concepts should be seen as avenues scarcely explored to date in foreign-language teaching. And yet they hold great promise for individualized instruction committed to serving differentiated goals based on individual students' aptitudes and attitudes.

In a general way, the concentration required for efficient foreign-language activities, particularly in the early phases, speak to student-teacher contact more frequent than five times a week and less lengthy than the traditional 40 to 60 minute period.

I also endorse the economy and productivity (both for the teacher and the students) emerging from a time arrangement that facilitates working with groups of different sizes: combined classes meeting for a prolonged period to see a movie; shorter periods conducted by a single teacher aimed at an initial presentation or explanation; smaller groups involved in discussion and/or demonstration of proficiency in using language in a face-to-face situation; individual students working with a tutor or a machine with a view to remediation or enrichment.

More important, if we take seriously the task of accommodating students inclined toward a single rather than a multiple-skill approach in exploiting physiological as well as cognitive aptitudes, we must consider seriously the potential of providing an opportunity for the students to move sequentially through a series of time modules whose content is dedicated to improvement of a single skill or subskill. Other students may pursue several language skills concurrently in additional modules. Such arrangement has implication not only for instruction but also for more realistic evaluation of student performance since a student's "grade" in one skill area would not be contaminated by performance or lack of performance in another skill. The flexible arrangement provides opportunity for all students to recoup from the effect of fragmentation through group activities dedicated to utilization of whatever skill or skills they have been developing.

In these somewhat grandiose plans for manipulating time slots, student groups, and teaching assignments, one must remain sensitive to student reactions. In 1961 we attempted in a modest way to implement a pilot program involving team teaching, flexible groups, and a degree of staff differentiation with a group of entering high-school freshmen. At the end of the first year we were reasonably satisfied with the results and planned to continue the students in a comparable program the second year. They asked for a meeting and presented their opposing position: although they were aware of the benefits accrued to them through the past year, because of our teaching structure they felt they could no longer respond positively. Each student wanted one teacher to whom he or she could relate personally in terms of instruction, evaluation, and counseling.

CHART 4

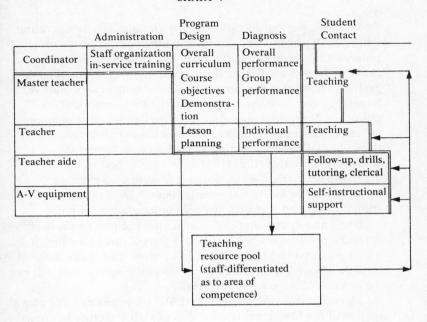

	Administration	Program Design	Diagnosis	Student Contact
Coordinator	Staff organization in-service training	Overall curriculum	Overall performance	
Master teacher		Course objectives Demonstration	Group performance	Teaching
Teacher		Lesson planning	Individual performance	Teaching
Teacher aide				Follow-up, drills, tutoring, clerical
A-V equipment				Self-instructional support

Teaching resource pool (staff-differentiated as to area of competence)

Time-Group Size Distribution
(determined by performance as related to personal objectives)

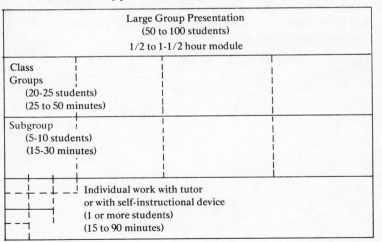

Large Group Presentation (50 to 100 students) 1/2 to 1-1/2 hour module			
Class Groups (20-25 students) (25 to 50 minutes)			
Subgroup (5-10 students) (15-30 minutes)			
Individual work with tutor or with self-instructional device (1 or more students) (15 to 90 minutes)			

Given proper consideration for the "human" factor operating among both students and teachers, a judicious institution of programs involving manipulation of time and personnel resources promises to improve the quality of instruction on several scores. Staff differentiation implies a better-coordinated curriculum in terms of program design, realistic goals, and appropriate objectives. It provides opportunity for the development of more effective ancillary materials and more student participation through small group activities. We see, as most important to student performance, the identification of the best-qualified diagnostician on the "team" capable of setting up effective prescriptions for individual remediation achieved through specially designed activities in a class or laboratory setting.

Last, the very fact that each teacher has options, on the basis of training and preference, to teach in the skill area for which he is best prepared and to work with group sizes most appropriate to his style is bound to increase the quality of the exposure as well as the morale of both students and staff.

The accompanying model (chart 4) is proposed as an approximation of the functional relationship of staff structure to group sizes. It is essential to keep in mind that the time element and the size of the group is to be staff-determined, depending on the nature of the content as regulated by diagnostic assessment. It is not to be construed as an inflexible, everyday pattern for instructional activities.

10

Far from the Cutting Edge

Curriculum

An overview of the foreign-language literature in the past generation reveals few attempts to relate foreign-language instruction to any broad curriculum model. The foreign-language curriculum is generally the province of the subject-matter specialist. His tentative objectives are subject-oriented and, except for a reaffirmation of faith in the value of foreign-language instruction, he seldom grapples with the intricate philosophical and organizational complexities inherent in legitimizing a coherent, total instructional pattern.[1]

It might be said that the emphasis to date has been primarily on a system of instruction rather than on a systematic curriculum and that, until recently, the system of instruction has focused on the design of materials (as approved by a consultant psychologist and linguist), which expressed a point of view, pious hope, and promised to be effective without contradiction provided the teacher faithfully adhered to the overelaborate directions of class activities supplied by the basal text.

This gross oversimplification of curriculum concerns, the imposition of a theoretical, mechanistic theory from on high without due concern for the teacher as vital to the instructional process and for the accepting child, a nonperson assumedly ready and able to justify the theory through his performance, probably has been an important factor in developing resistance to "New Key" ideals and procedure. It has been considered by some not only as threatening but as amoral.

The recent frenzy, stimulated by threats of "accountability," to measure programs more accurately through the development of performance criteria or behavioral objectives is certainly a move in the right direction. It is to be deplored, however, that the process to date has been more frustrating than illuminating. The writer of objectives usually vacillates between overgenerality dealing with the four accepted skills and the horrendous prospect of specifying content and testing conditions and defining acceptable performance. He is often self-conscious about working at the lower levels of the cognitive scale and overanxious to "work in" some measures that would reflect optimum changes on the upper limits of the affective scale.[2]

While completely supportive of the notion of clarifying objectives as a way to accountability and better-focused instruction, I am apprehensive that, in a climate of euphoria, the task of setting objectives becomes an end in itself rather than a means, a partial measure that may or may not produce a significant rearrangement of the multiple and complex factors impinging on the learning process.

Testing one skill by use of another (assumedly mastered) skill in the test item is another frequent pitfall that poses problems peculiar to evaluation in foreign-language courses. More seriously, there is little evidence in the flurry to develop behavioral objectives that any serious thought has been given to arriving at a fundamental position for developing the objectives. The process usually stems from a predisposition to a method of instruction or to a personal preference in terms of what skill is most important and what sequence is superior.[3] Little, if any, attention is paid to the capacity of the instructional staff to meet any given objective or to the complex problems that reaching a given objective may present for the learner in terms of talent, resources, time available, and disposition to the subject in general or to any of its component parts.

In other words, behavioral objectives of themselves can be destructive in proportion to their validity if their purpose is simply to evaluate (select, eliminate) in the traditional, punitive sense. However, they are prerequisite tools to measure individual progress if used at the formative stage for accurate diagnosis and at the summative stage for objective confirmation of having reached a mastery level in any educative activity.[4]

Let us elaborate on the Mastery Learning concept since it

provides an ideal framework for the type of individualization discussed previously. As first conceptualized by Carroll[5] and eventually refined by Bloom,[6] the Mastery Learning model, simply stated, assumes a normal distribution of aptitudes and proposes that by modifying the kind and quality of instruction and the amount of time available for learning the majority of students will achieve mastery in terms of the objectives set for a given task. Based on the observation that aptitude measures are more predictive of the rate of learning than of the level or complexity of learning possible, the model serves as justification for exposing all students initially to a given subject.

It is possible to consider individual aptitudes not only in terms of a global approach to a subject but also in relation to the student's capacities to handle subcomponents of the subject. This further refinement facilitates the notion of "ability to understand instruction" set as a prerequisite to Mastery Learning since this implies the development of instructional modes that the student accepts as particularly appropriate to his aspirations and talents. Furthermore, when coupled with the staff differentiation notion previously discussed, instruction becomes more individualized through exercising the diagnostic function in terms of proper choice of activities, media, group size, and so on, as indicated by diagnostic progress tests.

It has also been indicated in an earlier section that skill fragmentations, the concept of working with a discrete corpus of materials, provides a simplified base for setting up objectives on a two-dimensional scale involving skill development proficiency on one axis and vocabulary and structure loading on the other.

I should urge the structuring, within the framework of flexible scheduling, of activities and interventions initially congenial to the individual learner and subsequently extended to accommodate his learning rate rather than an arbitrary syllabus. I am confident that this procedure will result in the student's becoming, as a result of initial and continued success, a more efficient and persevering learner, first in his area of demonstrated strength and eventually in his approach to other language skills that originally seemed insurmountable to him.

In a broader vein, the consequences of applying the Mastery

Learning concept may be invaluable in stimulating and nurturing motivation. It relates directly to the argument that, given a number of students with no more than neutral attitudes toward foreign-language study, a proper system of instruction may indeed stimulate most to continue. Eventually, the word would probably get around that the foreign-language class provides an enjoyable, productive, and self-fulfilling experience. For lack of substantial precedents, the impact on enrollment is difficult to predict.

A major renaissance in the foreign-language field implies not only rethinking the mechanics of teaching and the role of learners as individuals; given the important role of the teacher as the implementing agent of the curriculum, serious consideration must also be given to the teacher's own attitude and the attitude of others toward the teacher.

If an improved sequence is to be a corporate venture, the staff involved must be treated with respect commensurate to the responsibilities it exercises. Rewards in terms of status, money, or other incentives must be available to encourage proper discharge of significant duties.[7] Insofar as harmonious interaction within the group is a key to efficient operation, participants in any phase of an innovative enterprise must be guided by canons provided by social psychology. If the chasm between theory and practice is to be bridged, teachers must be able to look at themselves as respected participants in and contributors to the curriculum process. If they are to be effective in terms of personal as well as collegial projects, they must be able to deal with the complexities of their peer group as well as with the dynamics of the classroom.[8]

Teachers must exchange a stance of insularity for a developing image as creative contributors. On the basis of objective evidence, they must question the stereotype of the teacher as the dispenser of gratuities and the center of activities. While becoming increasingly sensitive to the learner, they must see themselves as an essential resource within the classroom and resist the facile expedient of abrogating the responsibilities incumbent on them by dint of expertise. They must become respectful and trustful of the individual student, teach him to direct his own learning, and provide appropriate guidance so that he will share his experiences with his peers and make significant contributions to the morale and progress of the group.

Teachers must be nurtured to assume this new role. Their advice, reactions, and insights must be credited as relevant to the curriculum enterprise. A survey of curriculum models indicates that, characteristically, the flow of information is indicated by arrows pointing from the expert as designer to the child as consumer. Let us suggest a modification of the model reflecting concomitant responsibilities by indicating that the flow occurs in both directions. In such a model the teacher and child become originators as well as receptors of relevant data.

Teachers must be convinced that, in assuming the new role, the restraints they are accepting will be largely balanced by the additional personal freedom implied in the new image. The recent past has demonstrated that, in practically all subject areas, imposition of theoretical tenets from "above" has been generally rejected or sabotaged at the grass roots level, that arrogant domination does not constitute sufficient motivation for sustained, systematic support at the classroom level.

In short, teachers, most of whom are eager to learn, must be taught with concern for aptitudes, sensibilities, and individual orientation. Paternalism, authoritarianism, capricious decisions, and expedient, oppressive measures are no more appropriate to the teacher as an adult learner than to the child to whom he is ministering.

Research

Research, indispensable to our modern age, is of crucial importance to the field of education in general and to foreign-language instruction in particular. Previous pages have, wherever possible, referred to significant research reflecting an impressive arsenal of evaluative tools, sophisticated designs, and objective findings.[9] Also, where the research is highly technical and discipline-specific, the profession has taken vast strides to explicate and synthesize, to extrapolate the message essential if the practitioner is to convert theory into new conceptual bases for improved instruction.

We are, therefore, anticipating a continuation and acceleration of research.[10] Basic research addressing itself to absolute measurement will and must continue. It is important to reach definitive conclusions on the relative merits of one methodology over another, on the degree of function or dysfunction of one medium over another. It is equally essential to establish normative bases for individual student achievement in the several language skills. Continuing research into the native-language learning process with its implications for second-language learning must be accelerated.

I wish, however, to underline a number of supplementary directions that, at this time, might prove of direct benefit to foreign-language instruction, specifically to data that can contribute to immediate transformations at the instructional level. The possibility of utilizing research as a means of redesigning or modifying existing programs will depend to a great extent on the nature of the research. If, as in the past, research continues to consist principally of summative evaluation, that is, assessing the success or failure of a program at some terminal point by using the classic control group versus experimental group design, then the product of research will have limited influence on program implementation. Terminal findings will have terminal consequences: the program will continue if effective or be discontinued if ineffective.

If educators anticipate and encourage a shift to formative evaluation, a less rigorous design consisting of continuous, periodic assessment of the program measured in terms of degrees to which it meets its own objectives, there is the possibility of more effective intervention at appropriate points in the program.

I have indicated throughout this study, particularly in the sections dealing with psychology and linguistics, that, while a vast amount of knowledge is available, many questions important to the process of teaching and learning have not been answered or, in many cases, have never seriously been asked. These, specifically with reference to language experience, are often of a seemingly pedestrian nature. Nevertheless, they suggest several criteria for action-oriented, classroom-centered research clustered under the general criterion of applicability, a dimension of essential importance to the practitioner.

1. *Effect of Foreign-Language Instructional Factors on the Learner*

There is a great need to document student reactions to various programs and activities, particularly with a view to individualizing instruction. The following unanswered questions are illustrative of the direction data-collecting might take:

a. What is the effect of "success" on motivation?

b. To what degree do individual aptitudes affect student response to various language skills?

c. For what category of students is rote-learning more acceptable or more repugnant?

d. What are the norms of expectation in rate of learning and retention for different categories of students?

e. What short-term rewards are effective to compensate for the long-range, cumulative nature of foreign-language learning?

f. In what way is "readiness" for the language experience determined? At what point is saturation reached? What is the proper amount of concentration at various levels?

2. *Relevance of Course Content*

a. What do students of different ages wish they could say in the foreign language?

b. What situational vocabulary would best encourage utilization of the foreign language outside the classroom in a real-life situation?

c. What confrontation techniques will force the student to utilize his language repertoire in "real" as opposed to "quasi" communication? At what point can this process be initiated? How can continued development be assured?

d. What "cultural" topics are most stimulating to students? What are the implications for lexical and structural control?

e. To what extent can humor, whimsy, and beauty be incorporated into the content of elementary instruction? With what success?

3. Programmatic Concerns

a. Can a minimal vocabulary and structure inventory be delineated? To what extent will it be relevant? To what extent will it be acceptable to the profession?

b. To what extent can content and methodology be "standardized" for a particular system to make possible any degree of vertical and horizontal articulation?

c. What comprehensive, descriptive inventories can be compiled to facilitate selection of equipment, self-instructional programs, and adjunct materials as these relate to the individualization of instruction?[11]

The teacher who is actively engaged in the curriculum is keenly interested in finding answers to these questions. In his quest for improving instruction, he is eager for a rational base to confirm his intuitions, for documentation that enables him to measure the success of his activities in comparison to the experience of other colleagues. Many teachers are willing and qualified to shift their roles from consumers of research to that of participants in the research process.

Heretofore, "research" has been considerd primarily the province of the researcher, expert in establishing sophisticated design, collecting hard data (usually empirical) that is processed through complicated techniques (often associated with the computer). Although in no way minimizing the importance of this type of study, I suggest that it can be supplemented by another means. The teacher, confident that his perceptions are accurate, sensitive to the numerous variables operating among the students whom he has learned to know well, takes responsibility for recording his observations (anecdotes, log). Such information, available from the total staff, can be summarized and analyzed. When observed behavior is checked against anticipated behavior, program changes can be immediately effected to remedy discrepancies between intent and achievement.

Sufficient flexibility must be provided in the system to facilitate modification as suggested by evaluation. This flexibility must be evident in both administration and teacher attitude.

Positive response from students must have priority over commitment to a text or to a personal philosophy.

Sufficient staff time must be provided to establish channels of communication, collect data, ponder the evidence, and plan modifications.

Essentially, much of this process is operative in our schools on an individual, idiosyncratic level. It could become truly effective in a setting where evaluation and intervention becomes a collective, systematic effort adequately supported in terms of in-service training and released time for the teachers. Under such conditions the teacher's status changes. He is not only an unconscious collector of disparate data. He becomes a utilizer of data relevant to the kind of decision-making that leads to continuous review and improvement of the program.

Teacher participation may be so organized to have significance beyond the local level. To this effect a professional structure needs to be provided for the teacher, as prime collector of "live" data, that will give his efforts direction and will supplement his own admitted technical inadequacies. Supplied with a design and with instruments appropriate to a problem, many teachers will respond positively by participating in a serious investigation, particularly if they see the problem as relevant to their needs and are assured that the findings will be shared with them.

If feedback from the teacher is valued by the researcher (as well as the curriculum designer), the teacher must be convinced that his contribution is valuable. It must be accepted without condescension that the teacher's contribution will be more idiosyncratic than systematic, more sporadic than continuous, more intuitive than speculative. The teacher's reluctance to do research and publish in the scholarly tradition should be neutralized and he should be provided with other channels and formats of communication not excluding anecdotal reports, informal, descriptive materials, case studies, and so on.[12]

The sensitive and massive task of organizing the practitioner as part of total effort may at this point seem staggering. But given the multiplication of data sources thus created, the teacher's influence in identifying problems that need urgent answers and the eventual prospect of bridging the gap between theory and practice is a task that may well warrant our total commitment in human and financial resources. The entire field of education is becoming increasingly concerned with the gap existing between theory and practice:

The relationship between theory and practice must constantly be kept within the same field of vision in order for both to cope with the exigencies of reality. We have developed a substantial body of theory and certainly a rich body of practice, but somehow our failure has been to provide the transformations and bridging between the two. Kurt Lewin, one of the intellectual forebears of this volume, was preoccupied with this issue of the relationship between the abstract and concrete. He once compared this task to the building of a bridge across the gorge separating theory from the full reality. "The research worker can achieve this only if, as a result of a constant intense tension, he can keep both theory and reality fully within his field of vision."[13]

The challenge calls for a major revision of the function of research:

Research, armed with these data, might eventually become sufficiently sophisticated to anticipate educational communication network changes. Based on their work and subsequent recommendations, existing agencies might be altered, new ones established, new roles brought into being, and so forth. If researchers succeed in these efforts they will have harnessed some salient dimensions of educational knowledge diffusion for the first time in the field's history.[14]

The radical nature of the change to be affected precludes facile and immediate revisions. The foreign-language profession no less than any other members of the teaching corps might ponder the implications of the following quotation:

A synergy refers to the cooperative interaction of the various elements of a system. The underlying principle further provides that the gains of coordinated action are greater than the sum of the independent efforts of the separate elements. Because schools are a complex amalgam of many parts, geared for the achievement of identifiable outcomes, they ought properly to be synergies. That is, they ought to be organizations in which the targets and the battle tactics are both clear and acceptable to each of the parts, in which the capacities of each are fused into a powerful thrust toward the goals, and in which the separate parts, through collaborative function, acquire a potency otherwise impossible.

Schools, it must be said, are rarely synergies. The image of the school as a unified enterprise in which the participants support one another in the pursuit of common objectives is somewhat counterfeit.[15]

11   Cautious Optimism

My hope is that the preceeding chapters have left no doubt that, in recent years, foreign-language study has been in the mainstream of American education. The movement shared in the tendency to expand, in the climate of ferment and optimism, in the security of sufficient financial support from the federal and local levels. Conversely, such shortcomings and limitations as have been noted along the way are also attributable to the tenor of the times. Let us review them briefly by way of identifying a number of caveats that the educational enterprise and the foreign-language leadership might well consider for the future.

A few syndromes apparently permeate the American psyche, which are evident on television as well as in more sophisticated intellectual fields of operation. In each case, we can draw parallels between the "tube," foreign-language instruction, and general educational trends.

1. The panacea syndrome: association with an idealized image eliminates all problems grounded in reality. *TV*: "There was I in my Maidenform Bra." *F.L.*: With the "New Key" firmly in hand (and FLES blossoming, and enrollments increasing) bilingualism is ensured with resultant progress toward international communication and world peace. *Ed.*: A plethora of panaceas superseding each other with dizzying rapidity. We cite among others team teaching, modular scheduling, inquiry, simulation, the school without walls.

2. The white hat syndrome: by definition all who are not "good guys" are contemptible scoundrels. *TV*: The cult of the western hero with infinite extensions. *F.L.*: All audio-lingual precepts are good. Conversely, use of native idiom is taboo, translation sinful, vocabulary learning obscene, and "grammar" heretical. *Ed.*:

Reports of continuous shoot-outs between the various critics of
the schools and abject "traditionalists," between the champions
of relevance and the unrepenting exponents of subject matter,
between the serene theorist and the stubborn practitioner.

3. The part-for-the-whole syndrome: a single corrective
neutralizes all related problems or unrelated problems. *TV.*:
Coca Cola—it's the real thing. *F.L.*: The students uniformly
incapable of resisting the dialogue and structure drills as presented by a new breed of uniformly inspired and effective teachers
shall inevitably perform at a consistently high level. Skinner says
so. *Ed.* : The propensity for idyllic fantasies typified by the projection of unanimous student response in a climate of self-determination encouraged by liberated teachers operating infinitely
flexible facilities.

4. The science syndrome: research shows . . . *TV*: All products
are superior to all other competitive products and vice versa. *F.L.*:
Given a linguist, a psychologist, and a statistician (assisted
slightly by a superteacher), all materials will be foolproof. The
function of research will be to attest to the efficacy of these
materials as a testimonial to the "method." *Ed.:* The fixation on
elegant research design with a sometimes cavalier estimate of the
purpose of the research and the·significance of the findings to
assumedly related instructional problems. Obscurantism may be
noted as a subsyndrome since obfuscation plays no little part in
putting "science" beyond the grasp of the consumer: superhydro-
chlorophyl, phonemics-graphemics, eupsichian.

5. The technology syndrome: recognition of the infinite capacities of the machine to supplant human activities. *TV*: Self-tuning
sets, computerized interests, better cars. *F.L.*: Laboratories, projectors, computers as instrumental to successful learning independent of available appropriate software. *Ed.*: Television,
teaching machines, video-recorder, computer, and, soon, Telstar.

6. The callousness syndrome: insensitivity to consequences.
TV: Assumption that public gullibility has no limits and that the
consumer's taste need not be respected: deodorants, feminine
hygiene. *F.L.*: As the product must be sold without concern for
human dignity, so must the method prevail at any cost. Teachers

must swallow their shattered pride and rush off to institutes to be "retreaded." *Ed.*: Contempt for the traditionalists, for the monolithic system, for obsolete goals, for conforming students permeates the avant-garde literature. The "teacher-proof" curriculum becomes a serious obsession.

The above allusions are at best approximate and, in some instances, caricatures. And yet, we find them often substantiated in the pronouncements of mandarins as disseminated in official journals. They are characteristic of visionary assaults to achieve instant progress without due concern for the complexities of reality and the arduous systematic labors necessary in effecting change.

Such excesses as here implied suggest a renewed focus on less sanguinary approaches to the process of necessary and salutary transformation:

1. The educational apparatus consists of a number of inter-related components, each indispensable to the process of converting conceptualization to improved learning condition, even for a single student. In this total process transmission is as important as creation. It involves the researcher, those responsible for "cognitive transfer," the teacher and the child, each operating under conditions appropriate to his needs, objectives, and capacities. Under ideal conditions, the "flow" of interaction should be from the student upward as well as from the "theoretician" downward. The total apparatus will be no more effective than its weakest component, which is to say, no hierarchical value can be set on the contributions of the respective components.

2. Insofar as the apparatus functions in time, increased attention needs to be paid to the problem of transition. A component of the total structure must exist to bridge the gap between futuristic visions and the harsh realities of the depressing present, between theory and practice, between aspiration and implementation. At least one agency must militate against apparent dichotomies, mitigate threatening conflicts, and see improved communication across entities of the educational spectrum as an imperative.

It is against this background that I suggest that consolidation rather than innovation may be indicated as a primary task in the immediate future. We have learned that riding the crest is an exhilarating but ephemeral venture. We are aware that students will no longer engage in foreign-language study out of a sense of tradition, that they will not sustain interest in the subject simply to conform to the expectations of the best-intentioned theories. Enrollment reflecting reaction to successive crisis situations is unpredictable, financial support for curriculum is fickle, determined as much by historical accidents and social conditions as by response to individual interests, capricious and esoteric as these sometimes may be.

An insistence on consolidation is not to be construed as anti-thetical to the spirit of innovation. The two positions (note the white-hat syndrome previously cited) are not mutually exclusive. Innovators will not and cannot be suppressed. We are simply setting priorities on the less dramatic task of providing a stable and dependable springboard for subsequent, more imaginative thrusts.

These sobering realizations that we are far from having reached the millennium have led me to focus on the student as perhaps holding the key to continuing foreign-language instruction in our schools. While countenancing the prospects of minimal enrollment, I have expressed confidence in the existence of a number of students intrinsically motivated (for whatever reason) to seek exposure to foreign-language instruction. Not only is the school obligated to respond to this demand but the foreign-language teacher in particular is responsible for making the initial and subsequent exposure productive and rewarding at least for this limited population.

The first task in achieving this goal is the removal of traditional constraints: a global, linear, unidirectional approach militates against any attempt to meet the needs and accommodate the competencies of individual students, each bringing to the task differing capacities for mastering various language skills, each seeking fulfillment through the command of a particular and legitimate aspect of language learning.

I propose that under such initial conditions the success so essential to continuing perseverance could be assured by considering the sequence of study not only as the accumulation of lexical and structural content but also as the incremental development of perfection in the process of practicing along lines predicated by specific skills and subskills.

This approach, which I term "modular," is prerequisite to working with clearly delineated tasks equally tangible to the teacher and to the student. As process becomes perfected the mechanics of language manipulation gradually will be replaced by more spontaneous language activities, first contrived and eventually creative.

Motivation might be further increased at the contextual level through a systematic effort to determine what situations are more meaningful for different people of different ages, through the revision of procedures for integrating language and culture, through the development of new opportunities for encouraging use of the foreign language as a functional tool at home, abroad, and through intercontinental channels of communication.

Flexible scheduling and differentiated staffing have been briefly outlined as proper apparatus for foreign-language instruction and Mastery Learning was discussed as illustrating a number of concepts well worth the serious consideration of those in the foreign-language profession intent on individualizing instruction to a greater degree.

The intention is to stimulate interest in practices that will sustain the interest of at least a portion of the school population through the required long sequence. The hope is that, to the extent that it is successful, such a system might serve as a base for subsequent improvement and that the students emerging from a differentiated sequence indeed might provide the positive testimonials necessary to extending the influence of foreign-language study as a rewarding academic experience.

In considering these broad orientations I have tried to indicate the complexity of the task, the need for interdisciplinary contributions, for increased rapprochement between exponents of education and subject matter, between theory and practice, between those working at the cutting edge and those engaged in wrestling the stubborn realities of the schools, between the ivory tower and the crucible.

Discharging responsibilities for translating these aspirations into systematic action must reflect a corporate as well as an individual commitment.

Professional organizations must continue to exercise leadership. At the national as well as on the local level they must continue to disseminate information, to explicate highly technical information, to condense and summarize what is needed as a broader knowledge base at the operational level. They must initiate studies that result in awareness of the need for commonality and provide the documents necessary to exploit common goals and common resources. They must design research and curriculum networks in which the teacher becomes a willing and significant contributor.

The individual teacher, however, must avail himself of the vast information available to him. He or she must sacrifice the security of insularity for the excitement of cross-disciplinary participation. He or she must explore the potential of flexibility and the excitement of ambiguity. He must prize his new role as diagnostician, resource person, and friend and take legitimate pride in his contributions to the common endeavor.

The most urgent calls to action are often abortive. The very magnitude of the task described serves to reduce those who should be involved to a state of resigned impotence. Preceding efforts to be comprehensive in the analysis of the current scene and the summation of general avenues open to those interested in improving the status of foreign-language studies, while initially inciting mild approval, may have been disarming to those agencies or individuals anxious for immediate involvement. For the purpose of encouraging commitment at the action level, I submit a number of priorities that seem both essential and feasible.

Two corporate projects require immediate attention.

1. The various AATs would do well to standardize the vocabulary and structure loading for various levels of instruction in

the respective languages. As indicated in a previous section, completion of this task is an imperative if articulation is to become a reality. It is also a prerequisite to the development of a rational testing program.

2. The ACTFL needs to intensify its effort to stimulate research and to disseminate findings that have direct implications for teachers of all languages in their daily struggle with problems of motivation. Let us refer again to the identification of content areas of high interest to different age groups and to specific strategies that prove effective in fostering success for individuals within a group. Teachers must be involved in and rewarded for their contributions to this program.

For those classroom teachers (and they are many) who are restive and anxious to be involved in new directions three simple steps are here suggested as preconditions to action:

1. A considered commitment to learning gradually to play a modified role calls for increased attention to diagnostics as a basis for structuring class activities. This implies a radical departure from the "contractual" arrangement under which the teacher brings to class most of the commitment and does most of the work while the students pacifically respond to minimal expectancies in involvement and effort.

2. The student's potential for self-direction, his capacity to become a partner in the teaching-learning process, must be accepted as a primary condition. The student's abilities (actual or developing) to understand the nature of a properly defined task, to control his efforts in mastering the task, and, eventually, to report on his success are assets that the teacher cannot overlook. Student participation and self-direction will determine the degree to which the teacher is "free" to redistribute his time in order to cope more effectively with other individuals or other class activities suggested by his own diagnosis.

A first, symbolic step in this direction might well be a new approach to record-keeping. The traditional grade book, to a great degree, reflects individual nonperformance and emphasizes the "spread" in performance between students, usually in global terms that defy identification as letter or number "grades" are viewed in retrospect. An individual chart on which each item represents a single task provides a better profile of achievement to the student responsible for keeping it up to date and to the teacher relying on it for diagnostics.

3. Each teacher, depending upon responsibilities and personal and institutional resources, is advised to determine the scope of his intended activities. For teaching as well as learning is a matter of individual capacities and predilections. Among the many suggestions offered in the preceding pages none is intended to be prescriptive to any individual or to any group since involvement must remain a matter of personal commitment. The chairman of a large, progressive department in an opulent school administered by a dynamic principal realistically may plan to rewrite and initiate a totally new program based on elaborate objectives, involving a multimedia approach and the radical manipulation of time and staff through modular scheduling and differentiated staffing.

The aspiring teacher working in a less fortunate situation (probably the rule rather than the exception) must adjust his objectives to his very real limitations. Yet the teacher who has considered points one and two moves in an innovative direction the day he provides even a single student with a clear statement of a single task, addressing itself to a specific skill or subskill, related or unrelated to the basal text. With little or no guidance, the student will demonstrate his ability to master the task and, eventually, to report on his measure of success.

Such a concrete, limited practice is indeed a legitimate approach to curricular change. For the pattern, once established, may be extended to include other students and, subsequently, to increase the proportion of time available to each student involved in the individualized instruction process. Such a cautious, realistic approach, in the long run, may be a model for other teachers with consequential impact on the total school.

Many of those still engaged in the teaching of foreign languages will read their own experiences, their past contributions, their perplexities and frustrations in some or all of the preceding pages. Though we may not have done as well as we wished, let us be comforted that our efforts were not lacking in vision, devoid of honor, or barren of rewards.

There are others, committed through conviction or temperament to a career in foreign languages, who may read these same pages with mixed feelings. This group is encouraged to read critically, to select and reject, to take nothing on faith, to use this text only as a springboard to continuing study. You will do no better than others have—and yet you must—unless constant inquiry, rigorous self-analysis, and a continuous quest for excellence become your way of life.

Appendix A

Topics of Annual Reports of the Northeast Conference

1954. *Foreign Language Teachers and Tests.* Hunter Kellenberger, editor.

1955. *Culture, Literature, and Articulation.* Germaine Brée, editor.

1956. *Foreign Language Tests and Techniques.* Margaret Gilman, editor.

1957. *The Language Classroom.* William F. Bottiglia, editor.

1958. *The Language Teacher.* Harry L. Levy, editor.

1959. *The Language Learner.* F. D. Eddy, editor.

1960. *Culture in Language Learning.* G. Reginald Bishop, Jr., editor.

1961. *Modern Language Teaching in School and College.* G. Reginald Bishop, Jr., editor.

1962. *Current Issues in Language Teaching.* William F. Bottiglia, editor.

1963. *Language Learning: The Intermediate Phase.* William F. Bottiglia, editor.

1964. *Foreign Language Teaching: Ideals and Practices.* George F. Jones, editor.

1965. *Foreign Language Teaching: Challenges to the Profession.* G. Reginald Bishop, Jr., editor.

1966. *Language Teaching: Broader Contexts.* Robert G. Mead, Jr., editor.

1967. *Foreign Languages: Reading, Literature, Requirements.* Thomas E. Bird, editor.

1968. *Foreign Language Learning: Research and Development.* Thomas E. Bird, editor.

1969. *Sight and Sound: The Sensible and Sensitive Use of Audio-Visual Aids.* Mills F. Edgerton, Jr., editor.

1970. *Foreign Languages and the 'New' Student.* Joseph A. Tursi, editor.

1971. *Leadership for Continuing Development.* James W. Dodge, editor.

1972. *Other Words, Other Worlds: Language in Culture.* James W. Dodge, editor.

Appendix B

Topics Treated in Annual Reports of the FLES Committee of the AATF

1961: The Supply, Qualifications, and Training of Teachers of FLES.

1962: Language Structures at FLES Level, Including Testing for Mastery of Structures.[1]

1963: The Correlation of a Long Language Sequence Beginning in the Elementary School.[1]

1964: Reading at the FLES Level.[1]

1965: Culture in the FLES Program.[2]

1966: FLES and the Objectives of the Contemporary Elementary Schools.[2]

1967: The FLES Student: A Study.[2]

1968: FLES: Projections into the Future.[3]

1969: The Three R's of FLES: Research, Relevance, Reality.[3]

1970: FLES: Patterns for Change.[3]

1971: FLES: Goals and Guides.[3]

1972: FLES: U.S.A.: Success Stories.[3]

[1] Available from National Information Bureau, 972 Fifth Avenue, New York, New York.
[2] Available from Chilton Books, 401 Walnut Street, Philadelphia, Pennsylvania.
[3] Available from MLA-ACTFL Materials Center, 62 Fifth Avenue, New York, New York.

Appendix C

Table of Contents: *The Britannica Review of Foreign- Language Education*

Foreign Language Instruction," Lorraine A. Strasheim.
3. "Behavioral Objectives and Evaluation," Florence Steiner.
4. "Strategies of Instruction for Listening and Reading," Gilbert A. Jarvis.
5. "Strategies of Instruction for Speaking and Writing," Alfred N. Smith.
6. "Curricula for Individualized Instruction," Gerald E. Logan.
7. "Media in Foreign Language Teaching," Jermaine D. Arendt.
8. "Language Learning Laboratory," W. Flint Smith.
9. "Recent Developments in the Training and Certification of the Foreign Language Teacher," Howard B. Altman and Louis Weiss.
10. "Classics: The Teaching of Latin and Greek and Classical Humanities," Gerald M. Erickson.
11. "TESOL," Bernard Spolsky.
12. "Trends in Foreign Language Enrollments," Richard I. Brod.

Volume 3, 1970

1. "Introduction and Overview: Pluralism in Foreign Language Education," Dale L. Lange.
2. "Pluralism in Foreign Language Education: A Reason for Being," Frank M. Grittner.
3. "Cultural Pluralism," Genelle G. Morain.
4. "Approaches to Bilingualism: Recognition of a Multilingual Society," Manuel T. Pacheco.
5. "Foreign Language Interdisciplinary Programs and Activities," Helen P. Warriner.
6. "Language Learning Processes," G. Richard Tucker and Alison d'Angeljan.
7. "Instructional Strategies in Foreign Language Learning and Teaching," Alan Garfinkel.
8. "Individualization of Foreign Language Learning: What Is Being Done," Ronald L. Gougher.
9. "In-service Programs in Foreign Languages at Elementary and Secondary Levels," Robert I. Cloos.
10. "Modern Foreign Language Teaching in the Uncommonly Taught Languages," Richard T. Thompson.

Notes

1. Transition

1. For the substance of and quotations in this section, we are indebted to George B. Watts, "The Teaching of French in the United States: A History," *French Review* 37, no. 1 (October 1963). Readers interested in the history of teaching other languages may wish to consult *Reports of Surveys and Studies in the Teaching of Modern Foreign Languages* (New York: Modern Language Association, 1961), especially "The Training of German in the United States from Colonial Times to the Present," by Edwin H. Seidel, and "The Teaching of Spanish in the United States," by Sturgess E. Leavitt. Also available: Albert Parry, *America Learns Russian*, (Syracuse: Syracuse University Press, 1967), and Joseph Fucilla, *Teaching of Italian in the United States* (New Brunswick: American Association of Teachers of Italian, 1967).

2. Algernon Coleman, *The Teaching of Modern Languages in the United States* (New York: Macmillan, 1929).

3. For a brief résumé see Steven Darian, "Backgrounds of Modern Language Teaching: Sweet, Jespersen and Palmer," in *Modern Language Journal* 13, no. 8 (December 1969): 545–50.

4. For an elaboration of this phenomenon see Joshua A. Fishman, ed., *Readings in the Sociology of Language* (The Hague: Mouton, 1968). Fishman's *Sociolinguistics: A Brief Introduction* (Rowley, Mass.: Newbury House, 1971) also relates directly to this problem.

5. Michael P. West, *Learning to Read Foreign Languages* (London: Longmans Green and Co., 1926) and *The Construction of Reading Materials for Teaching a Foreign Language* (London: Oxford University Press, 1927). A collegial effort to develop a "reading method" was initiated at the University of Chicago as early as 1920. For a description and evaluation see Otto F. Bond, *The Reading Method: An Experiment in College French* (Chicago: University of Chicago Press, 1953).

6. For example, George E. Vander Beke, *French Word Book* (New York: Macmillan, 1929); Frederick C. Cheydleur, *French Idiom List* (New York: Macmillan, 1929); Joseph Landy, *Graded French Word and Idiom Book* (Boston: D. C. Heath, 1938); Bayard O. Morgan, *German Frequency Word Book* (New York: Macmillan, 1928); Hayward Keniston, *A Standard List of Spanish Words and Idioms* (Boston: D. C. Heath, 1941); Henry H. Josselson, *The Russian Word Count and Frequency Analysis* (Detroit: Wayne State University Press, 1953).

7. Such typical grammars include William H. Fraser and J. Squair, *Standard*

French Grammar (Boston: D. C. Heath, 1901); Peter H. Hagbolt, *A Modern German Grammar* (Boston: Ginn and Co., 1921); and Charles H. Grandgent, *Italian Grammar* (Boston: D. C. Heath, 1915).

8. R. D. Cole, *Modern Foreign Languages and Their Teaching* (Yonkers-on-Hudson: World Book Co., 1931); revised by J. B. Tharp (New York: D. Appleton-Century, 1937). C. H. Handschin, *Modern Language Teaching* (Yonkers-on-Hudson: World Book Co., 1940) and *Modern Language Teaching in the United States* (Yonkers-on-Hudson: World Book Co., 1923).

9. See Louis G. Kelly, *25 Centuries of Language Teaching* (Rowley, Mass.: Newbury House, 1969), especially chap. 9, "Gradation," and the following pages: reading versus listening, p. 261; psychology and the direct method, pp. 305-6; teaching of culture, pp. 312-16; differentiation among learners, pp. 321-22; motivation, pp. 324-25; phonetics, p. 338; culture, p. 378; dialects, p. 381; general remarks, p. 405. Those convinced that "Plus ça change, plus c'est la même chose," who wish for a briefer documentation of their position may consult Harold Dunkel, "Language Teaching in an Old Key," *Modern Language Journal* 47, no.5 (May 1963): 203-10.

10. Walter Kaulfer, *Modern Languages for Modern Schools* (New York: McGraw-Hill, 1942), is a good example of a book with"New Key"ideas expressed in "Old Key" nomenclature.

11. Paul F. Angiolillo, *Armed Forces' Foreign Language Teaching* (New York: S. F. Vanni, 1947).

12. Frederick Agard and Harold Dunkel, *An Investigation of Second Language Learning* (Boston: Ginn and Co., 1948).

13. Harold Dunkel, *Second Language Learning*, Appendix B, pp. 191-92.

14. For the names of the participants in the conference see Harold Dunkel, *Second Language Learning*, Appendix B, "Report of the Committee," pp. 191-92.

15. The complete "Resolutions" are quoted in Harold Dunkel, *Second Language Learning*, Appendix B, "Report of the Committee," pp. 191-96.

16. According to Mario Pei, *Glossary of Linguistic Terminology* (New York: Anchor Books, 1966), "audio-lingual" is listed as "The combination of listening and speaking, the two basic language skills, and teaching designed to produce them" (Brooks). Synonym: Aural-oral.

17. William Riley Parker, *The National Interest and Foreign Languages*, 3rd ed., Department of State Pub. no. 7324 (Washington, D.C., 1962). Parker was executive secretary of the Modern Language Association from 1947 to 1956 and was responsible for directing the foreign-language program initiated in 1952. For his own appraisal of MLA activities in that period see "What's Past Is Prologue," *PMLA* 81, no. 2 (April 1956).

18. James B. Conant, *The Education of American Teachers* (New York: McGraw-Hill, 1963).

19. Earl J. McGrath delivered his address before the Central States Modern Language Association held in Saint Louis in May 1952. His support for introducing foreign-language instruction in the grades was further reflected in the Nation-

al Conference on the Role of Foreign Languages in American Schools held in Washington, D. C., in 1953.

20. At the annual meeting of the Modern Language Association in December 1956, Oliver J. Caldwell delivered an address entitled "A Trend in Tongues," which was widely publicized and focused the interest of the public on the need for increasing language competency in the United States.

21. John S. Diekhoff, *NDEA and Modern Languages* (Modern Language Association, 1965), p. 27.

22. One of the first such surveys is the *Reports of Surveys and Studies in the Teaching of Modern Foreign Languages* (New York: Modern Language Association, 1961). The twenty-one studies cover a wide range of topics: enrollment, curriculum, evaluation, etc.

23. The *ALM* material has since undergone major revisions. As an example of another major audio-lingual series we mention that published by Holt (*Ecouter et Parler, Entender y Hablar*, etc.), which also illustrates a team approach by authors having previously been directly or indirectly associated with the Office of Education.

24. For example, assistance for the Glastonbury material came to $1,097,000. Other assistance for the better-known languages came to $1,800,000. Money was also spent gradually on developing materials in so-called exotic languages and is periodically reported in the *Linguistic Reporter*. See, for example, supplement no. 4 (December 1960). See also Richard J. Lambert, "Patterns of Funding of Language and Area Studies," *Journal of Asian Studies* 30 (February 1971): 399–421.

25. See Alfred B. Hayes, *Language Laboratory Facilities*, Washington, OE 21024, Bulletin 1963, no. 37.

26. The institute program of the NDEA was first implemented in 1959. During the first five years there were 301 summer and academic-year institutes for secondary and elementary school teachers. Several studies of NDEA language institutes appear in *Hispania* 52, no. 3 (September 1969): "Ten Years of NDEA Language Institutes (1959-1968)," by Laurence Poston; "From NDEA to EPDA: Can We Improve?" by Theodore Andersson; "A Decade of NDEA Language Institutions," by Charles L. King; "An Institute Director Looks Back," by J. Roy Prince; "Wichita State University's Involvement in the NDEA Institute Program," by Eugene Savaiano.

27. Parts C and D of the Education Professions Act of 1967 authorized the EPDA (Educational Personnel Development Act), the purpose of which was to improve the quality of teaching and help meet critical shortages of trained personnel in elementary and secondary schools. EPDA was an extension of NEA, which in the previous decade had served the same function primarily through the funding of M.A.T. Programs (Master of Arts in Teaching). Another part of the NDEA, Title VI, authorized fellowships for studies in modern foreign languages uncommonly taught in the United States while the Fulbright Act (Title IV of the NDEA) authorized fellowship programs in French, German, Italian, and Peninsular Spanish. Its purpose was to help strengthen and expand facilities for graduate

study in the United States and help increase the supply of college teachers. *The MLA Guide of Federal Programs,* ed. Kenneth W. Mildenberger, 1969, has information on all types of Federal Assistance and is available from the MLA/ERIC, 62 Fifth Avenue, New York, New York 10011.

28. Title III of the NDEA provided, among other things, matching federal funds to state departments of education for use in administering their acquisitions program and for providing supervision activities in private and public elementary and secondary schools in science, math, and foreign languages. There are now state supervisors of foreign language in forty-seven states and four possessions. Their names appear periodically in *Foreign Language Annals.* See 5, no. 2 (December 1971) for a recent roster.

29. See "Qualifications for Secondary School Teachers of Modern Foreign Languages," *Bulletin of National Association of Secondary School Principals* 39, no. 214 (November 1955): 30–33. The document was reprinted in the golden anniversary issue of *Modern Language Journal* 50, no. 6 (October 1966): Appendix B.

30. *The Modern Foreign Language Teacher Study* of the Modern Language Association, with the support of the Carnegie Corporation, developed "Guidelines for Teacher Education Programs in Modern Foreign Languages" in cooperation with the National Association of State Directors of Teacher Education and Certification. They may be found in *PMLA* 81, no. 2 (May 1966): A-2 and A-3, or in the *Modern Language Journal* 50, no. 6 (October 1966): 20–41.

31. I refer to the "Modern Language Association Foreign Language Proficiency Tests for Teachers and Advanced Students" (Educational Testing Service, Princeton, N. J. 08540, 1961), a seven-battery test including areas on listening comprehension, speaking, reading, writing, applied linguistics, civilization and culture, and professional preparation. The battery is available in five languages: French, German, Italian, Russian, and Spanish. Different forms are available in each language. A 38-page descriptive booklet is distributed free of charge by Educational Testing Service. Several achievement tests are currently available. The "MLA Cooperation Foreign Language Tests" (Educational Testing Service; Nelson Brooks and Donald Walsh, project directors, 1961) provides separate measures of the four skills at two levels of achievement in French, German, Italian, Russian, and Spanish. Sample sets are available. Paul Pimsleur, "Foreign Language Proficiency Tests (1967)," is available from Harcourt Brace Jovanovich. These achievements tests are prepared for French, German, and Spanish for the first three levels of language study. Separate tests measure proficiency in listening (test 1), speaking (test 2), reading (test 3), and writing skills (test 4). Price and descriptive information available from publisher. Commercially available aptitude tests include: The "Carroll-Sapon Modern Language Aptitude Test (MLAT)" published in 1958 and 1959, available from the Psychological Corporation, 304 East 45th Street, New York 10017, and the "Pimsleur Language Aptitude Battery," 1966, available from Harcourt Brace Jovanovich, 757 Third Avenue, New York 10017.

32. We have in mind the following studies: Raymond F. Keating, *A Study of*

the Effectiveness of Language Laboratories (New York: Institute of Administrative Research, Teachers College, Columbia University, 1963), which generated (among others) a reply by Marilyn J. Conwell, "An Evaluation of the Keating Report," *The Bulletin of the National Association of Secondary School Principals* 48, no. 290 (March 1964): 104–15. See also four articles in *Modern Language Journal* 48, no. 4 (April 1964). George Scherer and Michael Wertheimer, *A Psycholinguistic Experiment in Foreign Language Teaching* (New York: McGraw-Hill, 1964). Philip D. Smith, Jr., and others, *A Comparison Study of the Effectiveness of the Traditional Audio-Lingual Approach to Foreign Language Instruction Utilizing Laboratory Equipment* (also known as the "Pennsylvania Study") (Washington: U. S. Department of Health, Education, and Welfare, 1969). Each of these studies caused much ink to flow. For instance, an entire issue of the *Modern Language Journal* was devoted to the Pennsylvania Study, 53, no. 6 (October 1969). All of these studies were disappointing, particularly in the sense that the findings were not overwhelmingly conclusive with respect to the effectiveness of "New Key" practices.

33. See John B. Carroll, "Wanted: A research basis for educational policy on Foreign Language Teaching," *Harvard Educational Review* 30 (1960): 128–40. Paul Pimsleur, *Psychological Experiments Related to Second Language Learning: Report on the NDEA Conference* (Los Angeles: University of California, 1959). Albert Valdman, *The Implementation and Evaluation of a Multiple-Credit Self-Instructional Elementary French Course* (Indiana University, 1965), Multilith.

34. Note the following Office of Education brochures available from the U. S. Government Printing Office in the early 1960s: Marjorie C. Johnston, Ilo Remer, and Frank Sivers, *Modern Foreign Languages: A Counselor's Guide*, U. S. Department of H.E.W., O.E.-27004, Bulletin 1963, no. 37; Ilo Remer, *Handbook for Guiding Students in Modern Foreign Languages*, O.E.-77018, Bulletin 1963, no. 26; Marjorie Johnston and Elizabeth Keesee, *Modern Foreign Languages and Your Child*, O.E.-07020, Bulletin 1964.

2. Retrospect

1. Francis W. Nachtmann, executive secretary of the AATF, reports a growth in membership from 3,990 in 1954 to 11,100 in 1971. Following is a listing of professional organizations and publications important to the teacher of modern languages:

The American Association of Teachers of French, *The French Review*. Francis W. Nachtmann, University of Illinois, Urbana. Six issues per year, $8.00, $4.00 for students.

The American Association of Teachers of German, *The German Quarterly*. National Office: 339 Walnut Street, Philadelphia, Pa. 19106. $10.00.

The American Association of Teachers of Spanish and Portuguese, *Hispania*. Eugene Savaiano, secretary treasurer, Wichita State University, Wichita, Kansas 67208. Five issues per year, $8.00.

The American Association of Teachers of Italian, *Italica*. Ernest S. Falbo, secretary treasurer, Gonzaga University, Spokane, Washington 99202.

The American Association of Teachers of Slavic and East European Languages, *The Slavic and East European Journal*. Journals Dept., University of Wisconsin Press, Box 1397, Madison, Wisconsin 53706. Quarterly, $10.00.

The American Council on the Teaching of Foreign Languages, *Foreign Language Annals*. ACTFL, C. Edward Scebold, executive secretary, 62 Fifth Avenue, New York 10011. $6.50.

National Federation of Modern Language Teachers Association, Inc., *Modern Language Journal*. Wallace G. Klein, business mgr., 13149 Cannes Drive, Saint Louis, Mo. 63141. Eight issues per year, monthly Sept. through May, $5.00.

The Modern Language Association of America, *Publications of the Modern Language Association* (PMLA). George L. Anderson, treasurer, 4 Washington Place, New York 10003. 5 issues per year, $25 for regular membership, $7.00 for students.

2. I am thinking, as one instance among many, of the *Modern Language Journal* published under the auspices of the National Federation of Modern Language Teachers Association, particularly under the vigorous editorial leadership of Robert Roeming from 1962 to 1970. For testimonial articles to Roeming see *MLJ* 55, no. 1 (January 1971). Also *MLJ* 55 (March 1971).

3. We cite, as examples, the Skytop Lodge Colloquium on Curricular Change: Foreign Languages, held 2–5 April 1963 under the auspices of the College Entrance Examination Board (see *MLJ* [May 1963], p. 210, for a brief report) and the numerous conferences held in connection with the teacher preparation study under the leadership of F. André Paquette, which eventually resulted in a series of recommendations and guidelines publicized in a special issue of the *MLJ* 50, no. 6 (October 1966).

4. The Northwest Conference on the Teaching of Foreign Languages has met yearly since 1954. For a listing of the themes treated to date see Appendix A. The Kentucky Foreign Language Conference initiated in 1947 is, by now, a well-established institution; see *MLJ* 45, no. 1 (January 1961). The yearly Southern Conference and Central States Conference have more recently been instituted as additional forums for professional discussion. *FL Annals* publishes periodic lists of meeting dates for the various professional groups. See, for instance, *FL Annals* 4, no. 4 (May 1971), 370–71.

5. The National FLES Committee of the AATF has disseminated a yearly *Report* since 1961. For a list of topics see Appendix B.

6. For a listing of bulletins, newsletters, etc., reflecting foreign-language activities at the state and local levels, see *FL Annals* 5, no. 2 (December 1971): 183–86.

7. The Modern Language Association (and the National Federation of Modern Language Teachers Associations) cosponsored the establishment of the American Council on the Teaching of Foreign Languages in 1966. The purpose of the organization is to "promote study, criticism, and research in modern languages and their literatures, and to further the common interests of teachers of those sub-

jects." It is devoted to the problem of foreign-language teaching at all levels. For specifics as to the institution of ACTFL see *MLJ* 51, nos. 3, 5, 6 (March, May, October 1967).

8. ERIC, The Educational Resources Information Center, is a nationwide information system sponsored by the U. S. Office of Education. The ERIC Clearinghouse on the Teaching of Foreign Languages, located at 62 Fifth Avenue, New York 10011, processes all documents dealing with the teaching of the commonly taught languages—French, German, Italian, Russian, Spanish, Latin, and Greek. The ERIC Clearinghouse on Linguistics and the Uncommonly Taught Languages, housed at the Center for Applied Linguistics, 1717 Massachusetts Avenue, N.W., Washington, D. C. 20036, processes information on all other languages including English for speakers of other languages. Monthly résumés on all current accessions of ERIC are published in *Research in Education*, available from the U.S. Government Printing Office. ERIC documents of interest to foreign-language teachers are published in the ACTFL Annual Bibliography [*FL Annals*] which also indicates the source, cost, and form of such documents (microfiche, clothbound).

9. Mildred R. Donoghue, *Foreign Languages and the Elementary School Child* (Dubuque: W. C. Brown, 1968). Among others, the following books have been of inestimable help to FLES teachers: Marguerite Eriksson, Ilse Forest, and Ruth Mulhauser, *Foreign Languages in the Elementary School* (Englewood Cliffs, N. J.: Prentice-Hall, Inc., 1964); Mary Finocchiaro, *Teaching Children Foreign Languages* (New York: McGraw-Hill, 1964); Theodore Andersson, *Foreign Language in the Elementary School* (Austin: University of Texas Press, 1969).

10. Nelson Brooks, *Language and Language Learning: Theory and Practice* (New York: Harcourt, Brace, 1960). Robert Lado, *Language Testing* (London: Longmans, 1961) and *Language Teaching* (New York: McGraw-Hill, 1964). Following are some of the handbooks that have proved useful to foreign-language teachers: Theodore Huebener, *How to Teach Foreign Languages Effectively*, rev. ed. (New York: New York University Press, 1965). Robert Politzer, *Language Learning: A Linguistic Introduction* (Englewood Cliffs, N.J.: Prentice-Hall, 1965, 1970). Albert Valdman, ed., *Trends in Foreign Language Teaching* (New York: McGraw-Hill, 1966). Joseph Michel, ed., *Foreign Language Teaching* (New York: Macmillan, 1967. Wilga M. Rivers, *Teaching Foreign-Language Skills* (Chicago: University of Chicago Press, 1968). Frank Grittner, *Teaching Foreign Languages* (New York: Harper and Row, 1969). Peter F. Oliva, *The Teaching of Foreign Languages* (Englewood Cliffs, N. J.: Prentice-Hall, 1969). Kenneth Chastain, *The Development of Modern Language Skills: Theory to Practice* (Philadelphia: Center for Curriculum Development, 1971).

11. Elton Hocking, *Language Laboratory and Language Learning*, 2d ed., monograph no. 2, Department of Audio-visual Instruction, National Education Association of the U. S., 1967. Available from DAVI, NEA, 1201 Sixteenth Street, N.W., Washington, D. C. 20036. $4.50.

12. Rebecca M. Valette, *Modern Language Testing: A Handbook* (New York: Harcourt, Brace and World, 1967).

13. *Britannica Review of Foreign Language Education*, vol. 1, ed. Emma M. Birkmaier (Chicago: Encyclopaedia Britannica, Inc., 1968). *Britannica Review of Foreign Language Education*, vol. 2, ed. Dale Lange (1969). *Britannica Review of Foreign Language Education*, vol. 3, ed. Dale Lange (1970). I have not cross-referenced topics in this book with appropriate sections of the review. It is assumed that the reader, if he desires, can refer to the review's table of contents for further readings in areas of interest to him. The tables of contents are reproduced in Appendix C. It is most appropriate that Emma M. Birkmaier, known to the profession for her peerless leadership and indefatigable efforts, should have launched the *Britannica Review* as editor of the first volume.

14. Dr. Emile B. de Sauzé, former director of foreign languages in the Cleveland public schools, was personally responsible for the growth and success of the program. *The Cleveland Plan for the Teaching of Modern Languages with Special Reference to French* (Philadelphia: John C. Winston, 1920) illustrates teaching suggestions and lesson plans and gives evidence of the efficacy of the method.

15. Theodore Andersson made a major contribution in *The Teaching of Foreign Languages in the Elementary School* (Boston: D. C. Heath, 1953). The man and the book had tremendous influence in launching FLES as a major educational movement. His chapter, "The Teacher of Modern Foreign Languages," in *The Education of the Secondary School Teacher*, ed. E. Stabler (Middletown, Conn.: Wesleyan University Press, 1962), indicates the extent to which FLES was accepted as a permanent part of the curriculum.

16. FLES was heavily publicized in the early years. Under the leadership of Kenneth Mildenberger the Modern Language Association circulated a *F.L. Newsletter* in 1954 in which proper attention was given to FLES. Educational journals in many states reported the institution (and usually the success) of new FLES programs. Language journals provided a forum for discussing rationale, method, problems, and, in some cases, attempted to evaluate ongoing programs. FLES was also considered seriously by school administration and other educators. I was responsible from 1959 through 1963 for preparing an annotated bibliography for the *Elementary School Journal* in which the above comments are documented.

17. Theodore Andersson provides a model for adjusting instructional style to the students' level of maturation. See "The Optimum Age for Beginning the Study of Modern Languages," *International Review of Education* 6, no. 3 (1960): 303.

18. Wilder G. Penfield, *Speech and Brain Mechanisms* (Princeton: Princeton University Press, 1959).

19. Marjorie Breuning in *Report of Surveys and Studies* (1961) reports 1,227,000 students enrolled in FLES in 1959. By 1965 it was estimated that over two and one-half million students were studying foreign languages in the grades. It must be noted that these figures do not reflect the quality, quantity, or continuity of instruction.

20. The following articles reflect difficulties common to initiators of FLES programs:
Gloria W. Williams, "Pitfalls in Teaching Foreign Languages," *Chicago Schools Journal* 42 (October 1960): 26-29.

Jean V. Alter, "Potential FLES Teachers and Their Training," *Modern Language Journal* 46 (January 1962): 42–44.

"Foreign Languages for the Elementary School Teacher," *College of Education Record* 27 (January 1962): 21–25.

Doris T. Paine, "Who's to Teach My Child Foreign Language?" *Modern Language Journal* 41 (April 1962): 171–73.

John A. Carpenter, "American Schools Abroad: A Source of Language Teachers," *Modern Language Journal* 47 (May 1963): 189–91.

Rosario B. Ziegler, "On Starting a FLES Program," *Hispania* 46 (March 1963): 144–45.

21. Theodore Andersson considers the short supply of qualified teachers as a still conspicuous weakness besetting the future of FLES. See *Foreign Languages in the Elementary School* (Austin: University of Texas Press, 1969), p. 183.

22. It is paradoxical that in the area of the speaking skills emphasized by FLES programs, little hard data is available to measure achievement. My experience reported in Harold B. Dunkel and Roger A. Pillet, *French in the Elementary School* (Chicago: University of Chicago Press, 1962), reflects the conviction that FLES is a productive educational experience but also stresses the problems of individual differences and emphasizes the long hard road to limited competency.

23. In 1965 I compiled a follow-up study of the elementary school population as they finished high school. By that time, due to mobility, only eleven samples

PERCENTILE RANK OF STUDENTS
FOR VARIOUS NUMBERS OF SEMESTERS

Student Code Number	Freshman June 1961 SEMESTERS 2-4-6	Sophomore June 1962 SEMESTERS 4-6-8	Junior June 1963 SEMESTERS 6-8	Senior February 1964-June 1964 SEMESTERS Mid-8–end-8
3-20	99-99-89	99-95-78	99-94	99-99
3-21	99-86-47	98-84-54	99-94	99-99
3-22	99-86-47	97-78-45	99-94	85-92
3-23	91-51-12	93-64-29	99-94	85-92
3-24	88-43-9	81-39-11	56-22	63-87
3-25	83-35-6	96-72-37	99-90	90-95
3-26	71-21-2	86-47-16	31-10	no test
3-27	55-11-x	74-31-7	92-78	85-92
3-28	Residence in France	95-64-31	99-94	94-96
3-29	71-21-22	91-62-27	39-15	71-88
3-30	47-8-x	no test	4-x	x-45

were available. As measured by the somewhat inappropriate French Cooperative Test (Educational Testing Service, Princeton, N.J.), the percentile ranks in the freshman year indicate that most students registered success when measured in terms of two semesters, but that only three (3-20; 3-21; 3-22) can be said to have reached mastery in terms of four semesters of achievement. It may be noted that during the junior year most students achieved above the 75th percentile in terms of eight semesters and that practically all students were of the 85th percentile by the end of the senior year. These results point to the fact that maximum achievement is a function of length of exposure as well as a matter of starting age and/or methodology.

24. The best-intentioned guidelines, Appendix N, "Teacher Preparation for FLES," *Modern Language Journal* 50, no. 6 (October 1966): 95–99, for instance, if interpreted as being narrowly prescriptive, may interfere with a developmental approach to any program. In many cases, excellence is advanced as a criterion for beginning a program rather than as a goal to be achieved at the end of a thoughtfully planned experience.

25. We see evidence of this posture in Nancy B. Alkonis and Mary A. Brophy, "A Survey of FLES Practices," *Reports of Surveys and Studies in the Teaching of Modern Languages, 1959–1961* (New York: Modern Language Association), pp. 213–17.

26. For an elaboration of this notion see Roger A. Pillet, "The Impact of FLES: An Appraisal," *Modern Language Journal* 52, no. 8 (December 1968): 486–90.

27. A broader concern for student reactions is the theme of the *1967 Report of the FLES Committee of the AATF* entitled "The FLES Student: A Study."

28. There is more informal than formal evidence that the FLES instructor, as well as his high-school counterpart, has gradually shifted to the so-called eclectic approach in which each blends his personal views of traditional and audio-lingual.

29. See, for example, Gladys C. Lipton, "To Read or Not to Read: An Experiment in the FLES Level," *Foreign Language Annals* 3 (December 1969): 241–46.

30. See Virginia Spaar's report, "FLES in Retrospect," in "The FLES Student: A Study," a report by the FLES Committee of the American Association of Teachers of French (28 December 1967), Miami, Florida, pp. 97–124.

31. For a discussion of articulation as vital to FLES see Roger A. Pillet, "Prospects for FLES," *Advances in the Teaching of Modern Languages*, ed. G. Mathieu (Oxford: Pergamon Press, 1966), 2: 196–210.

32. Documentation on enrollment is provided by Richard I. Brod in *Britannica Review* 2: 341–62.

3. Assessment

1. Charles C. Fries, *Structure of English* (New York: Harcourt, Brace and Co., 1952), p. 4.

2. Charles A. Ferguson, ed., *Linguistic Reading Lists* (Washington: Center for Applied Linguistics, 1963).

3. M. A. K. Halliday et al., *The Linguistic Sciences and Language Teaching* (Bloomington: University of Indiana Press, 1964) and W. F. Mackey, *Language Teaching Analysis* (Bloomington: University of Indiana Press, 1965).

4. Simon Belasco, ed., *Anthology for Use with a Guide for Teachers in NDEA Language Institutes* (Boston: D.C. Heath, 1961).

5. We cite in the Heath Series: A. Valdman, *Applied Linguistics: French;* J. Marchand, *Applied Linguistics: German;* D. Cardenas, *Applied Linguistics: Spanish*; T. Magner, *Applied Linguistics: Russian*; R. Hall, *Applied Linguistics: Italian*; and in the Contrastive Structure Series, Charles A. Ferguson, ed. (University of Chicago Press): F. B. Agard and R. J. DiPietro, *The Sounds of Italian* (1965) and *The Grammatical Structures of English and Italian* (1965); W. G. Moulton, *The Sounds of English and German* (1962); H. L. Kufner, *The Grammatical Structures of English and German* (1962); R. P. Stockwell and J. D. Bowen, *The Sounds of English and Spanish* (1965) and *The Grammatical Structures of English and Spanish* (1965).

6. For instance, Robert Politzer, *Teaching French* (Boston: Ginn, 1960), *Teaching Spanish* (Boston: Ginn, 1961), and *Teaching German* (Wallhorn: Blaisdell, 1968).

7. The following are illustrative of attempts to interpret theory to practitioners: William G. Moulton, "Applied Linguistics in the Classroom," *PMLA* 76 (May 1961). Robert L. Politzer, "On the Relation of Linguistics to Language Teaching," *MLJ* 42 (February 1958). Albert Valdman, "From Structural Analysis to Pattern Drill," *French Review* 34 (December 1960). Norman P. Sacks, "Some Aspects of the Application of Linguistics to the Teaching of Modern Foreign Languages," *MLJ* 68 (January 1964). Robert L. Politzer, "The Impact of Linguistics on Language Teaching: Past, Present and Future," *MLJ* 68 (March 1964).

8. Fernand Marty, *Language Laboratory Learning* (Wellesley: Visual Publications, 1960), p. 33.

9. Quoted from Gustave Mathieu, "Pitfalls of Pattern Practice: An Exegesis," *Modern Language Journal* 47, no. 1 (January 1964). In the same issue see also Robert Politzer, "Some Reflections on Pattern Practice."

10. See Robert L. Politzer, *Foreign Language Learning* (Englewood Cliffs, N. J.: Prentice-Hall, 1970), pp. 140–41.

11. B. F. Skinner, "The Science of Learning and the Art of Teaching," *Harvard Education Review* 24 (1954).

12. See Kenneth Chastain, "A Methodological Study of Comparing the Audio-Lingual Habit Theory and the Cognitive Code Learning Theory," *Modern Language Journal* 52, no. 5 (May 1968) and 54, no. 6 (October 1970); also Simon Belasco, "C'est la guerre? Or Can Cognition and Verbal Behavior Co-exist in Second Language Learning?" *Modern Language Journal* 54, no. 6 (October 1970).

13. Robert J. Lambert, "Psychological Approaches to the Study of Language: On Learning, Thinking and Human Abilities," *Modern Language Journal* 47, no. 2 (February 1963) and "On Second Language Learning and Bilingualism," *Modern Language Journal* 47, no. 3 (March 1963).

14. David P. Ausubel, "Adults Versus Children in Second Language Learning:

Psychological Considerations," *Modern Language Journal* 48, (November 1964).

15. A number of important documents throw light on an area of prime importance to foreign-language learning. We cite Carroll's work (1958) formulating the dimensions of language aptitude: linguistic interest, associative memory, inductive ability, sound-symbol association, and verbal knowledge and follow-up work in this direction (Carroll, 1959; Carroll, 1962). Others explored the area of linguistic reasoning as a more important determinant to success than traditional IQ measures (Gardner-Lambert, 1965; Pimsleur, Stockwell, and Connie, 1962; Kingston and Bernard, 1967). Still others determined that motivation and perseverance were maximum factors in the language learning task (Gardner, 1959; Jakobovits, 1969: Spolsky, 1969).

16. Albert Valdman, "Toward a Better Implementation of the Audio-Lingual Approach," *Modern Language Journal* 54, no. 5 (May 1970).

17. See in particular chap. 2, "Acquiring Meaning: Second Language Learning," *Educational Psychology: A Cognitive View* (Holt, Rinehart, 1968), and chap. 4, "Second Language Learning," *School Learning: An Introduction to Educational Psychology*, with Floyd G. Robinson (New York: Holt, Rinehart, 1969).

18. Robert Gagné, *The Condition of Learning* (Chicago: Holt, Rinehart and Winston, 1965), particularly the chapter on "Sequence in the Learning of Foreign Languages." The hierarchy of performances involve: 1) signal learning, 2) stimulus-response learning, 3) chaining, 4) verbal association, 5) discrimination learning, 6) concept learning and 8) problem solving. An excellent illustration of the applicability is available in "Learning Hierarchies and Second-Language Reading" a paper delivered by Gilbert A. Jarvis at the 1971 Meeting of ACTFL in Chicago.

19. Jerome S. Bruner, *Process of Education* (Cambridge, Mass.: Harvard University Press, 1960), has had an important influence on educational thinking. I have found "The Function of Teaching," *Rhode Island College Journal* 1, no.2 (March 1960) and "The Act of Discovery," *Proceedings of the Sixteenth Annual Meeting of the Philosophy of Education Society* (1960) to be very helpful documents.

20. The numerous topics alluded to in this passage are comprehensive and provocatively treated by Leon A. Jakobovits, *Foreign Language Learning: A Psycholinguistic Approach* (Rowley, Mass.: Newbury House, 1970).

21. We see this generalization as applying to all disciplines and quote from Lee S. Shulman's "Perspectives on the Psychology of Learning and the Teaching of Science and Mathematics" (address to the American Association for the Advancement of Science, New York City, December 1968, p. 26). "Today, a developing, empirically-based psychology of learning for *homo sapiens* offers tremendous promise. But it can never be immediately translatable into a psychology of the teaching of mathematics or science. Mathematics and science educators must not make the mistake that the reading people have made and continue to make. The reason why the psychology of the teaching of reading has made such meager progress in the last twenty-five years is because they have insisted on being borrowers. Something new happens in linguistics and within three years a linguistic reading

series is off the press. It is an attempt to bootleg from one field and put directly into the other without the necessary intervening steps of careful empirical testing and research."

22. Goodwin Watson, *What Psychology Can We Trust?* (Bureau of Publications, Teachers College, Columbia University, 1961).

23. The three types of installation are usually referred to as audio-passive, audio-active, and audio-active-comparative. In addition to the works of Hocking, Iodice, and Marty previously cited, add Edward M. Stack, *The Language Laboratory and Modern Language Teaching*, rev. ed. (New York: Oxford University Press, 1966) and publications available from the U. S. Government Printing Office: Alfred S. Hayes, *Technical Guide for the Selection, Purchase, Use and Maintenance of Language Laboratory Facilities* (Office of Education, Bulletin no. 37, OE-21024, 1963), Joseph C. Hutchinson, *The Language Laboratory: How Effective Is It?* (Office of Education, OE-27021, 1964 and OE-27013, 1963).

24. My own experience with audio-visual presentation is reported in R. Pillet and F. Garrabrant, "French with Slides and Tapes," *Elementary School Journal* 62, no. 8 (May 1962), and R. Pillet, "French with Slides and Tapes—A Reappraisal," *Elementary School Journal* 65, no. 2 (November 1964).

25. For a succinct overview see Elton Hocking, "The Sound of Pictures," *Modern Language Journal* 52, no. 3 (March 1968) and "Technology in Foreign Language Teaching," *Modern Language Journal* 54, no. 2 (February 1970). See also his "Audio-visual Learning and Foreign Languages," in George E. Smith and M. Philip Lemon, eds., *Effective Foreign Language Instruction in the Secondary School* (Englewood Cliffs, N. J.: Prentice-Hall, 1969). For general information on audio-visual instruction see *Audio-Visual Instruction* 11, no. 8 (October 1966), an issue focusing on the relation of media to foreign-language instruction.

26. MPATI, initiated in 1960, was a visionary program involving nineteen universities in six states. Instructional programs were to be diffused by way of two DC-6's to participating schools over a wide geographical area. Technical problems, cost, scheduling, rigidity, and lack of adequate programs eventually contributed to the discontinuation of the effort.

27. The *Parlons Français* Series is a FLES program developed by Anne Slack for the modern language project for the public schools of Boston in 1961. It was eventually distributed by Heath de Rochemont.

28. The *Modern Language Journal* 49, no. 4 (April 1965) contains several articles on the use of TV in FLES instruction. For evaluative comments as to the effectiveness of instructional television see Earle S. Randall, "Research in Three Large Televised FLES Programs," *Modern Language Association FLES Packet* (New York: MLA, 1967).

29. For a list of programs available prior to 1966 Alfred I. Fiks, "Foreign Language Programmed Materials: 1966," *Modern Language Journal* 51, no. 1 (January 1967). Jacob Ornstein, "Programmed Instruction and Educational Technology in the Language Field: Boon or Failure?" *Modern Language Journal* 52, no. 7 (November 1968) discusses the past and the prospects of work in this field.

30. According to Patrick Suppes (with Max Junar), "Computer Assisted In-

struction," *NASSP Bulletin* 54, no. 343 (February 1970). The question is not whether computer-assisted instruction (CAI) will play an important role but when it will be forced to assume that role. Suppes further proposes that future national needs for such languages as Russian, Chinese, and Japanese will make it imperative to computerize courses in order to offset the lack of qualified teachers. In *Survey of Computing Activities in Secondary Schools*, final report (October 1970) of the American Institute for Research, Charles A. Darby found that in foreign-language instruction only 1.2 percent of schools listing each subject area use a computer. Darby also found dominance of computer applications by the math curriculum. In most of the schools surveyed, computer applications have been well integrated into the mathematics curriculum. Applications have rarely spread to other subject matters. See also Walton's article, "Computers in the Classroom: Master or Servant?" *NASSP Bulletin* 54, no. 343 (February 1970), for an introduction to jobs the computer can do for the teacher in the way of clerical work, as teacher's partner, etc. Also of interest is Peter S. Rosenbaum, "The Computer as a Learning Environment for Foreign Language Instruction," *Foreign Language Annals* 2, no. 4 (May 1969).

31. For the "File" and a general discussion of problems attending the teacher evaluation of culture see Lee Sparkman, ed., "Culture in the FLES Program," *1965 Report of the FLES Committee of the AATF* (Philadelphia: Chilton, 1966). See also Ernest H. Lewald, "A Tentative Outline of Problems in the Knowledge, Understanding of Cultures," *Modern Language Journal* 52, no. 5 (May 1968).

32. Among his many essays on culture note Nelson Brooks, "Teaching Culture in the Foreign Language Classroom," *Foreign Language Annals* 1, no. 3, (March 1968) and "Culture: A New Frontier," *Foreign Language Annals* 5, no. 1 (October 1971).

33. Howard Lee Nostrand, "Language, Culture and the Curriculum," in *Foreign Language and the Schools*, ed. Mildred R. Donoghue (Dubuque: William C. Brown, 1967). For a listing of some of Nostrand's impressive contributions in this area see *The Britannica Review* 1: 79.

34. Among numerous other articles see H. Ned Seelye, "Culture in the Foreign Language Classroom," *Illinois Journal of Education* 59, no. 3 (March 1968) and "Performance Objectives for Teaching Cultural Concepts," *Foreign Language Annals* 3, no. 4 (May 1970).

35. We call attention to Michel Beaujour and Jacques Ehrmann, "A Semiotic Approach to Culture," *Foreign Language Annals* 1, no. 2 (December 1967). For teachers of French in particular, Michel Benamou, *Pour une nouvelle Pédagogie du Texte Littéraire* (Paris: Hachette, 1972), and the resources available from the Educational Research Council of America (Rockefeller Building, Cleveland, Ohio 44113) under the direction of M. James R. Willard. I should also like to mention articles in *Le Français dans le Monde,* particularly no. 72 (April-May 1970) and no. 73 (June 1970) and no. 65 (June 1969).

36. The topic of kinesics is comprehensively treated in Jerald R. Green, "A Focus Report: Kinesics in the Foreign Language Classroom," *Foreign Language Annals* 5, no. 1 (October 1971).

37. Some of these limitations are reflected in the *Proceedings* of a Pre-Conference Workshop on Culture held in November 1971 under the auspices of the American Council in the Teaching of Foreign Languages.

38. T. Macirone, *Practical French Phonetics* (Boston: Allyn and Bacon, 1921), pp. 7–8.

39. L. Clark Keating, "What the French Think of Us," *Modern Language Journal* 47, no. 5 (May 1963).

40. John B. Carroll, "Research on Teaching Foreign Languages," in N. L. Gage, ed., *Handbook of Research on Teaching* (Chicago: Rand McNally and Co., 1963). Other articles by Carroll relevant to research in foreign languages are: "Foreign Languages for Children: What Research Says," *National Elementary Principal* 39 (May 1960): 12–15; "The Contributions of Psychological Theory and Educational Research to the Teaching of Modern Foreign Languages," *Modern Language Journal* 49, no. 2 (May 1965): 273–81, which also appears in Albert Valdman, ed., *Trends in Foreign Language Teaching* (New York: McGraw-Hill, 1966), pp.93–106. See also "Research in Foreign Language Teaching: The Last Five Years," *Reports of the Working Committees, Northeast Conference on the Teaching of Foreign Languages* (MLA Materials Center).

41. Since the *Reports of Surveys and Studies in the Teaching of Modern Foreign Languages* (New York: Modern Language Association, 1961), occasional articles have appeared in *Foreign Language Annals*, notably Glen Willbern, "Foreign Language Enrollments in Public Secondary Schools, 1965," 1, no. 2 (March 1968); "Foreign Language Entrance and Degree Requirements in Colleges that Grant the B. A. Degree: Fall, 1966," 1, no. 1 (October 1967); Anthony Gradisnik, "A Survey of FLES Instruction in Cities over 300,000," 2, no.1 (October 1968). The December 1968 issue (vol. 11, no. 2) contains an editorial on "Foreign Language Requirements for the Ph.D." and two articles related to this topic: Albert Allen Bartlett, "The Foreign Language Requirement for the Ph.D.: A New Approach," and John L. D. Clark, "The Graduate School Foreign Language Requirement: A Survey of Testing Practices and Related Topics." Also in the same issue, Jean A. Perkins, "State Certification and Proficiency Tests: The Experience in Pennsylvania." In vol. 3, no. 2 (December 1969) see Julia G. Kant, "Foreign Language Registration in Institutions of Higher Education, Fall 1968." In vol. 4, no. 1 (October 1970) see Anthony Papalia, "A Study of Attrition in Foreign Language Enrollments in Four Suburban Public Schools."

42. See Leon A. Jakobovits, "Research Findings and Foreign Language Requirements in Colleges and Universities," *Foreign Language Annals* 2, no. 4 (May 1969) and John B. Carroll: "The Contributions of Psychological Theory and Educational Research to the Teaching of Foreign Languages," in Albert Valdman, ed., *Trends in Language Teaching* (New York: McGraw-Hill, 1966), pp. 93–106. Also, John Carroll, "The Prediction of Success in Intensive Foreign Language Training," in Robert Glazer, ed., *Training Research and Education* (New York: Wiley, 1965) and "Linguistic Relativity, Contrastive Linguistics, and Language Learning," *International Review of Applied Linguistics*, 1 (1963). Paul Pimsleur and R.G. Bonkowski, "The Transfer of Verbal Material across Sense Modal-

ities," *Journal of Educational Psychology* 52 (1961): 104–7. Paul Pimsleur, D. M. Sundland, and Ruth D. McIntyre, "Underachievement in Foreign Language Learning," *International Review of Applied Linguistics* 2 (1964): 113–50. W. E. Lambert, R. C. Gardner, H. C. Barik, and K. Tunstall, "Attitudinal and Cognitive Aspects of Intensive Study of a Second Language," *Journal of Abnormal and Social Psychology* 46 (1963): 358–68. W. E. Lambert and Leon Jakobovits, "Verbal Satiation and Changes in the Intensity of Meaning," *Journal of Experimental Psychology* 40 (1960): 376–83. Leon A. Jakobovits, "Mediation Theory and the Single State S-R Model: Different?" *Psychological Review* 78 (1966): 376–81; Leon Jakobovits and M. S. Miron, eds., *Readings in the Psychology of Language* (Englewood Cliffs, N. J.: Prentice-Hall, 1967); Leon A. Jakobovits, "A Functional Approach to the Assessment of Language Skills," *Journal of English as a Second Language* 4 (1969): 63–76; Jakobovits, "Implications of Recent Psycholinguistic Developments on the Teaching of a Second Language," *Language Learning* 18 (1968): 89–109; Jakobovits, "Second Language Learning and Transfer Theory: A Theoretical Assessment," *Language Learning* 19 (1969): 55–86; and Jakobovits, introduction to "Foundations of Foreign Language Teaching and Learning: Psychological Aspects," in Eberhard Reichmann, ed., *The Teaching of German: Problems and Methods*, National Carl Schutz Association, Teaching Aid Project (Philadelphia: Winchell Company, 1970), part 2, chap. 1.

43. See R. L. Politzer, "Student Motivation and Interest in Elementary Language Courses," *Language Learning* 5 (1953–54): 15–21. Also, Leon Jakobovits, "Motivation and Foreign Language Learning: Part A. Motivation and Learner Factors," *Report to the 1970 Northeast Conference on the Teaching of Foreign Languages.* The Illinois Foreign Language Attitude Questionnaire Forms S-1 and S2 can be found in this 1970 report.

44. These studies have been cited in n. 32, chap. 1.

45. For example, see the many articles appearing in *Foreign Language Annals* since its first date of publication in October 1967, notably the following: Rebecca M. Valette, "Laboratory Quizzes: A Means of Increasing Laboratory Effectiveness," 1, no. 1 (October 1967); A. Bruce Gaarder, "Beyond Grammar and beyond Drills," 1, no. 2 (December 1967); Victor E. Hanzeli, "Linguistics and the Language Teacher," 2, no. 1 (October 1968); Christina Paulston, "Structural Pattern Drills: A Classification," 4, no. 2 (December 1970).

46. Joseph M. Vocalo, "The Effect of Foreign Language Study in the Elementary School upon Achievement in the Same Foreign Language in the High School," *Modern Language Journal* 51, no. 8 (December 1967): 463–69. Evelyn Brega and John M. Newell, "High School Performance of FLES and Non-FLES Students," *Modern Language Journal* 51, no. 7 (November 1967): 408–11. Joseph Justman and Martin L. Naas, "The High School Achievement of Pupils Who Were and Were Not Introduced to a Foreign Language in the Elementary School," *Modern Language Journal* 40, no. 3 (March 1956): 120–23.

47. See, for instance, Guillermo del Olmo, "Professional and Pragmatic Perspectives on the Audio-lingual Approach: Introduction and Review," *Foreign Language Annals* 2, no. 1 (October 1968).

48. See n. 30, chap. 1.

49. Robert Lado, *Language Testing* (New York: McGraw-Hill, 1964).

50. Rebecca Valette, *Modern Language Testing: A Handbook* (New York: Harcourt, Brace and World, 1967).

51. Benjamin S. Bloom et al., *A Handbook on Formative and Summative Evaluation of Student Learning* (New York: McGraw-Hill,1971).

52. For a discussion of nineteen questionnaire forms designed by W. E. Lambert to measure attitudes (eleven for students and eight for parents) see Leon Jakobovits, *Foreign Language Learning* (Rowley, Mass.: Newbury House, 1970), pp. 260–317. Though the questionnaires were designed for Canadians, Jakobovits points out their adaptability to other foreign-language situations.

53. The importance of setting objectives and of testing in the affective as well as in the cognitive domain is evident in the work of Valette (see n. 50, above) and others. The dual focus is observable principally since the appearance of Benjamin S. Bloom, *Taxonomy of Educational Objectives: Cognitive Domain* (New York: McKay, 1956) and a companion book, D. R. Krathwohl et al., *Affective Domain* (New York: McKay, 1964).

54. See James Hoetker, "The Limitations and Advantages of Behavioral Objectives in Arts and Humanities: A Guest Editorial," *Foreign Language Annals* 3, no. 4 (May 1970). Also Florence Steiner's two articles in *Foreign Language Annals*, "Performance Objectives in the Teaching of Foreign Languages," 3, no. 4 (May 1970), and "Teaching Literature by Performance Objectives," 5, no. 3 (March 1972).

55. These tests have already been mentioned in n. 31, chap. 1.

56. For a comparison of relative proficiency as measured by the MLA Foreign Language Proficiency Tests for Teachers and Advanced Students versus an absolute measure established by the Foreign Service Institute see John B. Carroll, "Foreign Language Proficiency Levels Attained by Language Majors Near Graduation from College," *Foreign Language Annals* 1, no. 2 (December 1967): 131–51, especially the charts between p. 141 and p. 151. The fundamental question raised is that of determining the kind of performance we wish to measure. Are we indeed determining normative achievement as related to course "content" or can we determine the degree to which students can cope in the second language using native proficiency as a determinant? See also Eugène Brière, "Are We Really Measuring Proficiency with Our Foreign Language Tests?" *Foreign Language Annals* 4, no. 4 (May 1971).

4. Educational and Professional Context

1. James B. Conant, *The Education of American Teachers* (New York: McGraw-Hill, 1963), pp. 84–85.

2. For an analysis of these trends see Bardwell L. Smith, "Educational Trends and the Seventies," *AAUP Bulletin* 56, no. 2 (June 1970).

3. Paul Olsen in *Reality and Relevance: Yearbook, 1969* (Washington: American Association of Colleges for Teacher Education, 1969), p. 41.

4. B. O. Smith et al., *Teachers for the Real World* (Washington: American Association of Colleges for Teacher Education, 1969), p. ix.

5. Ibid., pp. 130–31.

6. See n. 19, chap. 3 and our discussion (pp. 34–41) in the section on psychology. Given the dichotomy set up between rote-learning and inquiry, it is not surprising that Herbert Thelen in his *Education and the Human Quest* (New York: Harper, 1960) relegated foreign-language instruction to the skill-center as an activity peripheral to basic education.

7. John I. Goodlad, *School Curriculum in the United States* (New York: Fund for the Advancement of Education, 1964).

8. See Gertrude Moskowitz, "The Effect of Training Foreign Language Teachers in Interaction Analysis," *Foreign Language Annals* 1, no. 3 (March 1968); also her "Interaction Analysis—A New Modern Language for Supervisors," *Foreign Language Annals* 5, no. 2 (December 1971); and Mills F. Edgerton, Jr., "Training the Language Teacher—Rethinking and Reform," *Foreign Language Annals* 5, no. 2 (December 1971).

9. The substance of this section appeared under the title of "Demands of New Dimensions" in the *School Review* 73, no. 2 (Summer 1965). It is being reproduced, in part, with permission of the University of Chicago Press.

10. Charles A. Ferguson, ed., *Linguistic Reading List* (Washington, D. C.: Center for Applied Linguistics, 1963).

11. Joseph H. Greenberg, *Essay in Linguistics* (Chicago: University of Chicago Press, 1955).

12. Charles C. Fries, *Structure of English* (New York: Harcourt, Brace and Co., 1952), p. 7.

13. Raven I. McDavid, Jr., "Mencken Revisited," *Harvard Educational Review* 34, no. 2 (Spring 1964): 211–25.

14. Fries, *Structure of English*, p. 4.

15. For instance, William G. Moulton, "Applied Linguistics in the Classroom," *PMLA* 76 (May 1961); Robert L. Politzer, *Teaching French: An Introduction to Applied Linguistics* (Boston: Ginn and Co., 1960); and Albert Valdman, "From Structural Analysis to Pattern Drills," *French Review* 34 (December 1960): 170–81.

16. James S. Holton et al., *Sound Language Teaching* (New York: University Publishers, 1961); Fernand Marty, *Language Laboratory Learning* (Wellesley: Audio Visual Publications, 1960); Edward M. Stack, *The Language Laboratory and Modern Language Teaching* (New York: Oxford University Press, 1960).

17. *Modern Language Journal* 47 (October 1963).

18. *Modern Language Journal* 47 (December 1963).

19. Wilga M. Rivers, *The Psychologist and the Foreign-Language Teacher* (Chicago: University of Chicago Press, 1964).

6. Individualization

1. See "The FLES Student : A Study," *Report of the FLES Committee of the AATF, 1967*.

2. See "The Drop-Out of Students in High School Languages," *Report of the Northeast Conference, 1957.*

3. Foreign-language teachers have not been insensitive to the possibilities of manipulating instruction through various grouping strategies. As examples we cite Michael Hernick and Dora Kennedy, "Multi-Level Grouping of Students in the Modern Foreign Language Program," *Foreign Language Annals* 2, no. 2 (December 1968) and particularly, Percy Fearing, "Non-graded Foreign Language Classes: A Focus Report," *Foreign Language Annals* 2, no. 3 (March 1969). For a more general discussion of the impact of grouping see Phyllis R. Sweet and Ronald L. Nuttal, "The Effect of a Tracking System on Student Satisfaction and Achievement," *American Education Research Journal* 8, no. 3 (May 1971).

4. Concern for individualizing is the theme of *Modern Language Journal* 3 (October 1918). Individualized instruction was dominant in J. Lloyd Trump, *New Directions to Quality Education* (Washington: National Association of Secondary School Principals, 1956). That it remained a very live concern is evident from Willard J. Congreve, "Toward Independent Learning," and Robert J. Keller, "Toward Differentiated Instruction," both articles appearing in *North Central Association Quarterly* 37 (Spring 1963). See also David W. Beggs III and Edward G. Buffie, eds., *Independent Study: Bold New Venture* (Bloomington and London: Indiana University Press, 1965). National Society for the Study of Education, *Individualizing Instruction*, Sixty-first Yearbook of the Society, Part 1 (Chicago: University of Chicago Press, 1962). The applicability to foreign-language instruction was sketched in Roger A. Pillet, "Individualizing Instruction: Implication for FLES," *Bulletin of the Department of Foreign Languages* NEA, 5, no. 2 (1967). More recently, articles on the subject have proliferated. Among others: a series by John F. Bockman and Ronald L. Gougher, "Individualized Instruction," appearing in the following issues of *Foreign Language Annals* 4, no. 1 (October 1971), 4, no. 4 (May 1971), 5, no. 2 (December 1971), 5, no. 3 (March 1972). Robert L. Politzer, "Toward Individualization in Foreign Language Teaching," *Modern Language Journal* 55, no. 4 (April 1971) and Florence Steiner, "Individualized Instruction," *Modern Language Journal* 55, no. 6 (October 1971). A comprehensive survey of this area is available in Howard B. Altman and Robert L. Politzer, *Individualizing Foreign Language Instruction: Proceedings of the Stanford Conference* (Rowley, Mass.: Newbury House, 1971). A perceptive analysis of the trend is provided by Victor E. Hanzeli, "Foreign Language Teachers and the 'New Student': A Review Article," *Modern Language Journal* 55, no. 1 (January 1971).

5. See John F. Bockman, "The Process of Contracting in Foreign Language Instruction," in *Proceedings of the Stanford Conference*, cited in n. 4, above.

6. *Proceedings of the Stanford Conference*, p. 67.

7. I feel, as an illustration, that such books as John Holt, *How Children Fail* (New York: Pitman, 1964), tend to distort through overgeneralization.

8. For a discussion of the problems and an annotated bibliography see Benjamin S. Bloom, Allison Davis, and Robert Hess, *Compensatory Education for Cultural Deprivation* (New York: Holt, Rinehart and Winston, 1965).

9. William F. O'Neill, ed., *Selected Educational Heresies* (Chicago: Scott, Foresman, 1969), provides a generous sampling of the critics of the school.

10. As a case in point of this poignant conflict we cite J. T. Dillon, *Personal Teaching* (Columbus: Merrill, 1971).

11. See Mara Vamos and John Harmon, "Foreign Language Entrance Requirements in Colleges that Grant the B. A. Degree: Fall, 1966," *Foreign Language Annals* 1 (1967).

12. See Lorraine A. Strasheim, "The Anvil or the Hammer: A Guest Editorial," *Foreign Language Annals* 4, no. 1 (October 1970). The *1970 Report of the Northeast Conference* addresses itself to the topic "Foreign Languages and the 'New Student,' " Victor Hanzeli and William Love, eds., *New Teacher for New Students*, which summarizes the proceedings of a Seattle Symposium in 1970, available from the Modern Language Association Materials Center.

7. Priorities

1. The seriousness of the problem of articulation was identified early, as in Manuel H. Guerra, "New FLES Adventures and the Villain of Articulation," *Modern Language Journal* 42, no. 7 (November 1958). Constructive advice has not been in short supply. We cite "Continuum of Materials and Consistency of Techniques," *1963 Report of FLES Committee of AATF: A Six Year Program* (Grades 7–12), Raleigh, North Carolina State Board of Education, 1963 (ERIC Document No. ED-013581; Marguerite Eriksson et al., *Foreign Languages in the Elementary School* (Englewood Cliffs, N. J.: Prentice Hall, 1964); Everett V. O'Rourke, "Continuum in Language Learning," *Advances in the Teaching of Modern Languages* 2, ed. G. Mathieu (Oxford: Pergamon Press, 1966). For more recent views on the subject see Louise Couture, "French in the Birmingham (Michigan) Elementary Schools," *Foreign Language Annals* 2, no. 3 (March 1969) and Michael J. Moore, "The Articulation Jungle," *French Review* 44, no. 2 (December 1970).

2. A serious attempt to deal with high school to college articulation is exemplified by a series of conferences sponsored annually by the University of Illinois in Urbana. See Richard E. Spencer and Ronald L. Flaugher, "A Study of an Assumption about High School and College Equivalency in Language Training," *Modern Language Journal* 51, no. 6 (October 1967).

3. The issue of transposing new methods into the college curriculum has been discussed among others by Norman Sacks, "Training the New College Instructor," *Modern Language Journal* 50, no. 6 (October 1966) and by Archibald T. MacAllister, "The Preparation of College Teachers of Foreign Languages," *PMLA* 79, no. 2 (May 1964).

4. See guidelines for *Three Levels of Competence in French*, a report of the Bloomington Conference held in 1969 and disseminated by the State of Illinois Superintendent of Public Instruction.

5. *Le Français fondamental 1er Degré and 2eme Degré* compiled by the Ministère de l'Education Nationale and distributed by Chilton (1954) has long been available as an audio-lingual frequency list for French. My own efforts at establishing vocabulary common to children and adults have appeared as "French

Word List for the 'New Key,' " *French Review* 38, no. 2 (December 1964). Modern word lists in other languages are also available: J. Alan Pfeffer, *Grunddeutsch: Basic [Spoken] German Word List* (Englewood Cliffs, N. J.: Prentice-Hall, 1964); Rodney Swenson, *A Frequency Count of Contemporary Germon Vocabulary Based on Three Current Leading Newspapers, Final Report* (Minneapolis: University of Minnesota, 1967), OE Contract No. 3-7-068838-1576. Spanish: Alphonse G. Jilland and E. Chang-Rodriguez, *Frequency Dictionary of Spanish Words* (The Hague: Mouton, 1964). Russian: Nicholas P. Vakar, *A Word Count of Spoken Russian: The Soviet Usage* (Columbus: Ohio State University Press, 1966).

6. See Arno G. Preller, "Some Problems Involved in Compiling Word Frequency Lists," *Modern Language Journal* 54, no. 5 (May 1970).

8. Contributions Welcome

1. Dwight Bolinger, "The Theorist and the Language Teacher," and Victor H. Hanzeli, "Linguistics and the Language Teacher," are excellent examples of contributions in this direction. Both articles appear in *Foreign Language Annals* 2, no. 1 (October 1968).

2. We refer the reader to John W. Oller, Jr., "Transformational Theory and Pragmatics," *Modern Language Journal* 54, no. 7 (November 1970), and Robert Lado, "Language, Thought, and Memory in Language Teaching: A Thought View," *Modern Language Journal* 51, no. 8 (December 1970). For a more recent discussion of the issues see Karen R. Lewis, "Transformational-Generative Grammar: A New Consideration to Teaching Foreign Languages," *Modern Language Journal* 56, no. 1 (January 1972).

3. See n. 5, chap. 3.

4. See chap. 4 (pp. 88–111) in Wilga Rivers, *Teaching Foreign-Language Skills* (Chicago: University of Chicago Press, 1968).

5. For a comprehensive discussion of techniques see Pierre Léon, "Teaching Pronunciation" in Albert Valdman, ed., *Trends in Language Teaching* (New York: McGraw-Hill, 1966).

6. The various types of equipment and their functions are described in Alber J. Harris, *How to Increase Reading Ability* (5th ed.; New York: David McKay, 1970).

7. See n. 5, chap. 1.

8. See Rebecca Valette, "The Use of the Dictée in the Foreign Language Classroom," *Modern Language Journal* 48, no. 7 (November 1964).

9. See, among others, H. H. Stern,"First and Second Language Acquisition" in *Perspectives on Second Language Teaching* (Ontario: Modern Language Center Publications, no. 1, 1970).

10. John B. Carroll, "Current Issues in Psycholinguistics and Second Language Teaching," *TESOL Quarterly* 5, no. 2 (June 1971).

11. Preliminary findings from research in progress: Milton Finstein, University of Chicago.

12. See Young Kyu Whang, *The Interaction of Short-Term Memory and*

Instructional Variables on Verbal Ability. (Unpublished Ph.D. dissertation, Department of Education, University of Chicago, 1971).

13. The renewed interest in memorization (with a special chapter on mnemonics) is expressed in Donald A. Norman, *Memory and Attention* (New York: Wiley and Sons, 1969). See also Paul Pimsleur, "A Memory Schedule," *Modern Language Journal* 51, no. 2 (February 1967).

14. For a more detailed discussion of available hardware as listed in *The Audio-Visual Equipment Directory,* 19th ed. (Audio-Visual Association, Inc., 3150 Spring Street, Fairfax, Virginia, 1969), see our "Audio-Visual Equipment and Materials" in the *1970 Report of the FLES Committee of the AATF.* For an overview see Elton Hocking, "Technology in Foreign Language Teaching," *Modern Language Journal* 54, no. 2 (February 1970).

15. See n. 6, above.

16. John B. Carroll, "Memorandum: On Needed Research in the Psycholinguistic and Applied Psycholinguistic Aspects of Language Teaching," *Foreign Language Annals* 1, no. 3 (March 1968): 237. Dial-access, a promising means of disseminating individual programs, serves to illustrate the gap between technical resources and appropriate software available. Paucity of the latter inevitably reduces the multiplier effect of the most sophisticated electronic system.

17. While PLATO provides encouragement as a stimulating example of computerized instruction, it also indicates the complex process of preparing prototypes and the time lag between initial programs limited in scope and commercial distribution of numerous programs available in several languages. See Richard T. Scanlan, "Computer-Assisted Instruction: PLATO in Latin," *Foreign Language Annals* 5, no. 1 (October 1971).

18. Since earlier expressions of international faith in television (as exemplified by *Modern Language Teaching by Television* circulated by the Council for Cultural Cooperation of the Council of Europe, Strasbourg [1965], systematic efforts to exploit the medium have waned. This in spite of the fact that we may increasingly have to deal with visually oriented learners as is argued by Caleb Cattegno in his *Toward a Visual Culture: Educating Through Television* (New York: Outerbridge and Dienstfrey, 1969).

19. See Dwight Allen and Kevin Ryan, *Microteaching* (Reading, Mass: Addison Wesley, 1969), and Howard Altman and Arnulfo G. Ramirez, "Beyond Micro-Teaching: Some First Steps in Individualizing Pre-Service Training for Foreign Language Teachers," *Modern Language Journal* 55, no. 5 (May 1971). See also John Pierre Berwald, "The Videotape Recorded as a Teaching Aid," *French Review* 43, no. 6 (May 1970).

20. The recent national interest in performance contracting serves as a background for parallel developments in foreign-language instruction. Keeping in mind Baird Shuman's exhortations, "Let's Take Foreign Languages Out of Schools," *Modern Language Journal* 55, no. 1 (January 1971), we see concrete evidence of moving in this direction in the local press where an affiliate of Behavioral Research Laboratories is advertising: "Learn a Language and Like it or your money back."

9. New Directions

1. Language problems aside, the need to "update" cultural content is discussed by Elton Hocking in "Culture, Relevance and Survival," *Modern Language Journal*, 54, no. 8 (December 1970).

2. As an example we call attention to an attractive bilingual brochure, *Community College: Career Outlook*, pp. 71-72, circulated by the Program Development Service, Department of Manpower and Immigration, Ottawa.

3. Lyndon Harris, "The Teaching of Swahili," *Modern Language Journal* 52, no. 3 (March 1968).

4. Louise J. Hubbard, "Modern Languages for the Racially Disadvantaged," *Modern Language Journal* 52, no. 3 (March 1968).

5. I suggest, as a place to start, George R. Stewart, *Names on the Land* (Boston, Mass.: Houghton Mifflin, 1958).

6. For a discussion of grouping according to level of attainment rather than grade level see David W. Beggs III and Edward G. Buffie, *Nongraded Schools in Action: Bold New Venture* (Bloomington: Indiana University Press, 1969). In the context of foreign-language teaching see Percy Fearing, "A Focus Report on: Nongraded Foreign Language Classes," *Foreign Language Annals* 2, no. 3 (March 1969), and Ronald I. Terwilliger, "Multi-Grade Proficiency Grouping for Foreign Language Instruction," *Modern Language Journal* 54, no. 5 (May 1970). John A. Rallo describes a method of period regrouping of high-school students in "A Cooperative French Program: A New Approach," *Foreign Language Annals 2, no. 4* (May 1969). Interclass exchanges across the Atlantic made possible by technology are described by Sister Ruth A. Jonas, S.C., "The Twinned Classroom Approach to FLES," *Modern Language Journal* 53, no. 5 (May 1969). Also Fred H. Wood, "The McCluer Plan: Innovative Non-graded Foreign Language Program," *Modern Language Journal* 54, no. 3 (March 1970).

7. For an overview see David W. Beggs III, ed., *Team Teaching: Bold New Venture* (Bloomington: Indiana University Press, 1969). There is little evidence in the foreign-language journals to indicate how well this concept has been applied to foreign-language teaching.

8. See Donald C. Manlove and David W. Beggs III, *Flexible Scheduling Using the IndiFlex Model* (Bloomington: Indiana University Press, 1965). See also Dwight W. Allen and Robert L. Politzer, "Flexible Scheduling and Foreign Language Instruction: A Conference Report," *Modern Language Journal* 55, no. 5 (May 1967); see also Robert N. Bush and Dwight Allen, *A New Design for High School Education: Assuming a Flexible Schedule* (New York: McGraw-Hill, 1964).

9. See James L. Olivero and Edward G. Buffie, eds., *Educational Manpower: From Aides to Differentiated Staff Patterns* (Bloomington and London: Indiana University Press, 1970). For a shorter overview of the problem see James L. Olivero, "The Meaning and Application of Differentiated Staffing in Teaching," *Phi Delta Kappan* (September 1970). James M. Cooper, *Differentiated Staffing: New Staff Utilization Patterns for Public Schools* (Philadelphia: Saunders, 1971).

10. Far from the Cutting Edge

1. For recent overviews of direction in curriculum design and evaluation see Ralph Tyler, Robert Gagné, Michael Scriven, Robert Stake, and J. Stanley Ahman, "Perspectives of Curriculum Evaluation," *AERA*, Monograph Series (Washington: American Educational Research Association, 1967), and Michael Connelly, ed., *Curriculum Theory Network: Elements of Curriculum Development* (Ontario: Ontario Institute for Studies in Education, 1971).

2. The rash of "handbooks" emerging from publishers suggests the degree to which consumers are intent on setting up performance objectives, e.g., Robert F. Mayer, *Preparing Objectives for Programmed Instruction* (San Francisco: Fearon, 1962); Robert J. Armstrong et al., *Developing and Writing Behavioral Objectives* (Tucson: Educational Innovators Press, 1968); Normand Groolund, *Starting Behavioral Objectives for Classroom Instruction* (New York: Macmillan, 1970); John C. Flanagan et al., *Behavioral Objectives: A Guide to Individualizing Learning* (Palo Alto: Westinghouse Learning Corporation, 1971).

3. A case in point, the admirable attempt to establish common measurement instruction in Stanislaus County, California (*Teaching Spanish by Being Responsible for Specific Objectives*, mimeo, 1971) assumes that instruction will begin with exposure to understanding and speaking, which are prerequisite for testing proficiency in the other skills.

4. See Egon G. Guba, "The Failure of Educational Evaluation," *Educational Technology* (May 1969). Also, Bloom et al., *Handbook on Formative and Summative Evaluation*, particularly chaps. 4, 5, and 6.

5. John B. Carroll, "Model of School Learning," *Teachers College Record* 64 (1963).

6. See H. Block, ed., *Mastery Learning* (New York: Holt, Rinehart, 1971), for selected papers by Bloom, Carroll, and others, as well as an exhaustive annotated bibliography.

7. See Roger A. Pillet, "Teacher Training in Foreign Languages: An Overview," *Modern Language Journal* 54, no. 1 (January 1970).

8. As a "Refresher" to previous formal course work, we suggest continued attention in these areas through such readings as Goodwin Watson, "Resistance to Change," in *The Planning of Change*, ed. W.G. Bennis and others (New York: Holt, Rinehart, 1969), and Herbert Thelen, *Classroom Grouping for Teachability* (New York: Wiley Press, 1967).

9. Egon G. Guba and David L. Stufflebeam, *The Process of Stimulating, Aiding and Abetting Insightful Action* (Columbus: Evaluation Center, Ohio State University, 1968). Also Desmond Cook, *Program Evaluation and Review Technique* (Washington: Office of Education, 1966).

10. Much relevant research is in progress. For instance, the Stanford Center for Research and Development has already produced, under the leadership of Robert L. Politzer, a number of significant documents: *An Experiment in Improving Achievement in Foreign Language Through Learning of Selected Skills Associated with Language Aptitude*, (1969); *Characteristics and Behaviors of the Suc-*

cessful Foreign Language Teacher (1969). These and other titles are currently available through Rand-McNally, Chicago, Illinois. I know that this type of research effort is being continued in many universities and school systems. There is a problem in the fact that, while research findings are eventually published, no clearinghouse exists to indicate what research is actually in progress.

11. The amount and direction of progress in the last twenty-five years can be assessed if one compares the lists of questions currently pertinent and those proposed by the 1946 committee that were summarized earlier in this essay.

12. Bridging the gap between theory and practice and involving the teacher more actively in research procedures is given serious attention by Leon Jakobovits in his *Foreign Language Learning.*

13. W. G. Bennis, *The Planning of Change,* p. 4.

14. W. C. Wolf, "Knowledge Generation," *Educational Researcher* (January 1970), p. 27.

15. Louise J. Rubin, "Synergetics and the Schools," *Contemporary Thought on Public School Curriculum* (Dubuque: Brown, 1968), p. 19.

Bibliography

Adams, E. N., Morrison, H. W., and Reddy, J. M. "Conversation with a Computer as a Technique of Language Instruction." *MLJ* 52, no. 1 (January 1968).

Agard, Frederick B., and Di Pietro, R. J. *The Grammatical Structure of English and Italian.* Contrastive Structure Series. Charles A. Ferguson, general editor. Chicago: University of Chicago Press, 1965.

————. *The Sounds of English and Italian.* Contrastive Structure Series. Charles A. Ferguson, general editor. Chicago: University of Chicago Press, 1965.

————, and Dunkel, Harold. *An Investigation of Second Language Learning.* Boston: Ginn and Co., 1948.

Allen, Dwight W., and Politzer, Robert L. "Flexible Scheduling and Foreign Language Instruction: A Conference Report." *MLJ* 51, no. 5 (May 1967).

————, and Ryan, Kevin. *Microteaching.* Reading, Mass.: Addison-Wesley, 1969.

Alter, Jean V. "Potential FLES Teachers and Their Training." *MLJ* 46, no. 1 (January 1962).

Altman, Howard B., and Politzer, Robert L., eds. *Individualizing Foreign Language Instruction.* Proceedings of the Stanford Conference, 6-8 May 1971. Rowley, Mass.: Newbury House, 1971.

————, and Ramirez, Arnulfo G. "Beyond Micro-Teaching: Some First Steps in Individualizing Pre-service Training for Foreign Language Teachers." *MLJ* 55, no. 5 (May 1971).

Andersson, Theodore. *Foreign Languages in the Elementary School: A Struggle against Mediocrity.* Austin and London: University of Texas Press, 1969.

————. "From NDEA to EPDA: Can We Improve?" *Hispania* 52, no. 3 (September 1969): 357-61.

————. "The Optimum Age for Beginning the Study of Modern Languages." *International Review of Education* 6, no. 3 (1960): 303.

————. *The Teaching of Foreign Languages in the Elementary School.* Boston: D. C. Heath, 1953.

Note: The following abbreviations are used throughout:
MLJ: *Modern Language Journal*
FLA: *Foreign Language Annals*
PMLA: *Publications of the Modern Language Association*

Angiolillo, Paul F. *Armed Forces' Foreign Language Teaching*. New York: S. F. Vanni, 1947.

Armstrong, Robert J., et al. *Developing and Writing Behavioral Objectives*. Tucson: Educational Innovators Press, 1968.

The Audio-Visual Equipment Directory. 19th ed. Audio Visual Association, Inc., 3150 Spring Street, Fairfax, Virginia, 1969.

Audiovisual Instruction. Department of Audiovisual Instruction, National Education, 1201 16th Street, N. W., Washington, D. C. 20036. Published monthly except July and August.

Ausubel, David P. "Adults Versus Children in Second Language Learning: Psychological Considerations." *MLJ* 48, no. 7 (November 1964).

————. *Educational Psychology: A Cognitive View*. New York: Holt, Rinehart, 1968.

————, and Robinson, Floyd G. *School Learning: An Introduction to Educational Psychology*. New York: Holt, Rinehart and Winston, 1969.

Banathy, Bela. "The Systems Approach." *MLJ* 51, no. 5 (May 1967).

————, and Lange, Dale L. *A Design for Foreign Language Curriculum*. Lexington, Mass.: D. C. Heath and Co., 1972.

————, and Sawyer, Jesse O. "The Primacy of Speech: An Historic Sketch." *MLJ* 53, no. 8 (December 1969).

Barrutia, Richard. *Language Learning and Machine Teaching*. Philadelphia, Pa.: The Center for Curriculum Development, Inc., 1969.

Bartlett, Albert Allen. "The Foreign Language Requirement for the Ph.D.: A New Approach." *FLA* 2, no. 2 (December 1968).

Beaujour, Michel, and Ehrmann, Jacques. "A Semiotic Approach to Culture." *FLA* 1, no. 2 (December 1967).

Beggs, David W., III, ed. *Team Teaching: Bold New Venture*. Bold New Venture Series. Bloomington and London: Indiana University Press, 1969.

————, and Buffie, Edward G., eds. *Independent Study*. Bold New Venture Series. Bloomington and London: Indiana University Press, 1965.

————. *Nongraded Schools in Action*. Bold New Venture Series. Bloomington and London: Indiana University Press, 1969.

Belasco, Simon, ed. *Anthology for Use with a Guide for Teachers in NDEA Language Institutes*. Boston: D. C. Heath, 1961.

————. "C'est la guerre? Or Can Cognition and Verbal Behavior Co-exist in Second Language Learning?" *MLJ* 54, no. 6 (October 1970).

Benamou, Michel. *Pour une nouvelle pédagogie du texte littéraire*. Paris: Hachette, 1972.

Bennis, W. G., et al., eds. *The Planning of Change*. New York: Holt, Rinehart, 1969.

Berwald, John Pierre. "The Videotape Recorder as a Teaching Aid." *French Review* 43, no. 6 (May 1970).

Block, James H., ed. *Mastery Learning*. New York: Holt, Rinehart, 1971.

Bloom, Benjamin S., ed. *Taxonomy of Educational Objectives. Handbook I: Cognitive Domain*. New York: David McKay, 1956.

————, Davis, Allison, and Hess, Robert. *Compensatory Education for Cultural Deprivation*. New York: Holt, Rinehart and Winston, 1965.

————, Hastings, J. Thomas, and Madaus, George F. *Handbook on Formative and Summative Evaluation of Student Learning*. New York: McGraw-Hill, 1971.

Bockman, John F., and Gougher, Ronald L. "Individualized Instruction." *FLA* 4, no. 4 (May 1971).

————. "Individualized Instruction." *FLA* 5, no. 1 (October 1971).

————. "Individualized Instruction." *FLA* 5, no. 2 (December 1971).

————. "Individualized Instruction." *FLA* 5, no. 3 (March 1972).

Bolinger, Dwight. "The Theorist and the Language Teacher." *FLA* 2, no. 1 (October 1968).

Bond, Otto F. *The Reading Method: An Experiment in College French*. Chicago: University of Chicago Press, 1953.

Brega, Evelyn, and Newell, John M. "High School Performance of FLES and Non-FLES Students." *MLJ* 51, no. 7 (November 1967).

Brière, Eugène. "Are We Really Measuring Proficiency with Our Foreign Language Tests?" *FLA* 4, no. 4 (May 1971).

Britannica Review of Foreign Language Education 1-3. See Appendix C.

Brooks, Nelson. "A Guest Editorial: Culture—A New Frontier." *FLA* 5, no. 1 (October 1971).

————. "Teaching Culture in the Foreign Language Classroom." *FLA* 1, no. 3 (March 1968).

————, and Walsh, Donald, project directors. *The MLA Cooperative Foreign Language Tests*. Educational Testing Service, Princeton, N. J. 08540, 1961. Provides measure of the four skills at two levels of achievement in French, German, Italian, Russian, and Spanish. Sample sets are available.

Bruner, Jerome S. "The Act of Discovery." *Proceedings of the Sixteenth Annual Meeting of the Philosophy of Education Society, 1960*.

————. "The Function of Teaching." *Rhode Island College Journal* 1, no. 2 (March 1960).

————. *Process of Education*. Cambridge, Mass.: Harvard University Press, 1960.

Bush, Robert N., and Allen, Dwight W. *A New Design for High School Education: Assuming a Flexible Schedule*. New York: McGraw-Hill, 1964.

Cardenas, Daniel. *Applied Linguistics: Spanish*. S. Belasco, ed. Boston: D. C. Heath, 1961.

Carney, Helen K. "VOCAW and ECHO: Advertising Foreign Languages." *FLA* 4, no. 1 (October 1970).

Carpenter, John A. "American Schools Abroad: A Source of Language Teachers." *MLJ* 47, no. 5 (May 1963).

Carroll, John B. "The Contributions of Psychological Theory and Educational Research to the Teaching of Modern Foreign Languages." *MLJ* 49, no. 2 (May 1965). Also in Valdman, Albert, ed., *Trends in Foreign Language Teaching*. New York: McGraw-Hill, 1966.

————. "Current Issues in Psycholinguistics and Second Language Teaching." *TESOL Quarterly* 5, no. 2 (June 1971).

————. "Foreign Language Proficiency Levels Attained by Language Majors Near Graduation from College." *FLA* 1, no. 2 (December 1967).

————. "Foreign Languages for Children: What Research Says." *National Elementary Principal* 39 (May 1960).

————. *Language and Thought*. Englewood Cliffs, N. J.: Prentice-Hall, 1964.

————. "Linguistic Relativity, Contrastive Linguistics, and Language Learning." *International Review of Applied Linguistics* 1 (1963): 1–20.

————. "Memorandum: On Needed Research in the Psycholinguistics and Applied Psycholinguistic Aspects of Language Teaching." *FLA* 1, no. 3 (March 1968).

————. "Model of School Learning." *Teachers College Record* 64 (1963).

————. "The Prediction of Success in Intensive Foreign Language Training." In Glazer, Robert, ed., *Training, Research and Education*. New York: Wiley, 1965.

————. "Research in Foreign Language Teaching: The Last Five Years.: *Reports of the Working Committees, Northeast Conference on the Teaching of Foreign Languages*. Edited by R. G. Mead, Jr. New York: Modern Language Association Materials Center.

————. "Research on Teaching Foreign Languages." In *Handbook of Research on Teaching*. Edited by N. L. Gage. Chicago: Rand McNally and Co., 1963.

————. "Wanted: A research basis for educational polity on foreign language teaching." *Harvard Educational Review* 30 (1960): 128–40.

The Carroll-Sapon Modern Language Aptitude Test (MLAT). Psychological Corporation, 304 East 45th Street, New York, N. Y. 10017, 1958, 1959.

Cattegno, Caleb. *Toward a Visual Culture: Educating through Television*. New York: Outerbridge and Dienstfrey, 1969.

Chastain, Kenneth. *The Development of Modern Language Skills: Theory to Practice*. Philadelphia: Center for Curriculum Development, 1971.

————. "A Methodological Study of Comparing the Audio-Lingual Habit Theory and the Cognitive Code Learning Theory." *MLJ* 52, no. 5 (May 1968).

Cheydleur, Frederick C. *French Idiom List*. New York: Macmillan, 1929.

Clark, John L. D. "The Graduate School Foreign Language Requirement: A Survey of Testing Practices and Related Topics." *FLA* 2, no. 2 (December 1968).

————. *Foreign-Language Testing: Theory and Practice*. Philadelphia, Pa.: Center for Curriculum Development, Inc., 1972.

Cloos, Robert I. "A Four-Year Study of Foreign Language Aptitude at the High School Level." *FLA* 4, no. 4 (May 1971).

Cole, R.D., and Tharp, J.B. *Modern Foreign Languages and Their Teaching*. Yonkers-on-Hudson: World Book, 1931. Revised by J.B. Tharp. New York: Appleton-Century, 1937.

Coleman, Algernon. *The Teaching of Modern Foreign Languages in the United States*. New York: Macmillan, 1929.

Conant, James B. *The Education of American Teachers*. New York: McGraw-Hill, 1963.

Congreve, Willard J. "Toward Independent Learning." *North Central Association Quarterly* 37 (Spring 1963).

Connelly, Michael, ed. *Curriculum Theory Network: Elements of Curriculum Development*. Ontario: The Ontario Institute for Studies in Education, 1971.

Conwell, Marilyn J. "An Evaluation of the Keating Report." *The Bulletin of the National Association of Secondary School Principals* 48, no. 290 (March 1964): 104–15.

Cook, Desmond. *Program Evaluation and Review Technique: Applications in Education*. U. S. Department of Health, Education, and Welfare, Office of Education. U. S. Government Printing Office, 1966.

Cooper, James M. *Differentiated Staffing: New Staff Utilization Patterns for Public Schools*. Philadelphia: Saunders, 1971.

Cornfield, Ruth. *Foreign Language Instruction*. New York: Appleton-Century-Crofts, 1966.

Couture, Louise. "French in the Birmingham (Michigan) Elementary Schools." *FLA* 2, no. 3 (March 1969).

"Critique of the Pennsylvania Project." *MLJ* 53, no. 6 (October 1969).

Darian, Steven. "Backgrounds of Modern Language Teaching: Sweet, Jespersen and Palmer." *MLJ* 53, no. 8 (December 1969).

del Olmo, Guillermo. "Professional and Pragmatic Perspectives on the Audio-lingual Approach: Introduction and Review." *FLA* 2, no. 1 (October 1968).

Department of Manpower and Immigration, Ottawa. *Community College Career Outlook 71-72*. Information Canada. Ottawa, 1971. (In French and English.)

de Sauzé, Emile B. *The Cleveland Plan for the Teaching of Modern Languages with Special Reference to French*. Philadelphia: John Winston, 1920, 1924, 1946, 1953.

Diekhoff, John S. *NDEA and Modern Foreign Languages*. New York: Modern Language Association, 1965.

Dillon, J. T. *Personal Teaching*. Columbus: Merrill, 1971.

Donoghue, Mildred. *Foreign Language and the Elementary School Child*. Dubuque: W.C. Brown, 1968.

D'Ooge, Benjamin L. *Concise Latin Grammar*. Boston: Ginn and Co., 1921.

Dunkel, Harold. "Language Teaching in an Old Key." *MLJ* 47, no. 5 (May 1963).

————. *Second Language Learning*. Boston: Ginn and Co., 1948.

Edgerton, Mills F., Jr. "Training the Language Teacher: Rethinking and Reform." *FLA* 5, no. 2 (December 1971).

Educational Research Council of America. Rockefeller Building, Cleveland, Ohio 44113.

ERIC Clearinghouse on the Teaching of Foreign Languages, 62 Fifth Avenue, New York 10011.

ERIC Clearinghouse on Linguistics and the Uncommonly Taught Languages. 1717 Massachusetts Avenue, N. W., Washington, D. C. 20036.

Ericksson, Marguerite, Forest, Ilse, and Mulhauser, Ruth. *Foreign Languages in the Elementary School*. Englewood Cliffs, N. J.: Prentice Hall, Inc., 1964.

Fearing, Percy. "A Focus Report on: Nongraded Foreign Language Classes." New York: MLA/ERIC Focus Report 4, 1970. *FLA* 2, no. 3 (March 1969).

Ferguson, Charles A., and Stewart, William A., eds. *Linguistic Reading Lists for Teachers of Modern Languages*. Washington, D. C.: Center for Applied Linguistics, 1963.

Fiks, Alfred I. "Foreign Language Programmed Materials: 1966." *MLJ* 51, no. 1 (January 1967).

Finocchiaro, Mary. *Teaching Children Foreign Languages*. New York: McGraw-Hill, 1964.

Fishman, Joshua A., ed. *Readings in the Sociology of Language*. The Hague: Mouton, 1968.

"Foreign Languages for the Elementary School Teacher." *College of Education Record* 27 (January 1962): 21–25.

"Foreign Language Requirements for the Ph.D.: An Editorial." *FLA* 2, no. 2 (December 1968).

Fraser, William H., Squair, J. *Standard French Grammar*. Boston: D. C. Heath, 1901.

Fries, Charles C. *Structure of English*. New York: Harcourt, Brace and World, 1952.

Fucilla, Joseph. *Teaching of Italian in the United States*. New Brunswick, N. J.: Rutgers University Press. American Association of Teachers of Italian, 1967.

Gaarder, Bruce A. "Beyond Grammar and Beyond Drills." *FLA* 1, no. 2 (December 1967).

Gagné, Robert. *The Conditions of Learning*. New York: Holt, Rinehart and Winston, 1965.

Garfinkel, Alan. "Stanford University Conference on Individualizing Foreign Language Instruction, May 6-8, 1971." Academic Report. *MLJ* 55, no. 6 (October 1971).

Goodlad, John I. *School Reform in the United States*. New York: Fund for the Advancement of Education, 1964.

Goodwin, Watson, "Resistance to Change," in Bennis, W. G., Benne, K. D., and Chin, R. *The Planning of Change*. New York: Holt, Rinehart and Winston, Inc., 1969.

Gradisnik, Anthony. "A Survey of FLES Instruction in Cities Over 300,000." *FLA* 2, no. 1 (October 1968).

Grandgent, Charles H. *Italian Grammar*. Boston: D. C. Heath, 1915.

Green, Jerald R. "A Focus Report: Kinesics in the Foreign Language Classroom." *FLA* 5, no. 1 (October 1971).

Greenberg, Joseph H. *Essays in Linguistics*. Chicago: University of Chicago Press, 1955.

Grittner, Frank M. "A Focus Report: Maintaining Foreign Language Skills for the Advanced Course Dropout." *FLA* 2, no. 2 (December 1968).

―――. *Teaching Foreign Languages*. New York: Harper and Row, 1969.

Groolund, Norman. *Stating Behavioral Objectives for Classroom Instruction*. New York: Macmillan, 1970.

Guba, Egon G. "The Failure of Educational Evaluation." *Educational Technology* (May 1969).

Guerra, Manuel H. "New FLES Adventures and the Villian of Articulation." *MLJ* 42, no. 7 (November 1958).

"Guidelines for Teacher Education Programs in Modern Foreign Languages." *PMLA* 81, no. 2 (May 1966): A-2 and A-3. Also in *MLJ*, golden anniversary issue 50, no. 6 (October 1966): 20–41.

Hagbolt, Peter H. *A Modern German Grammar*. Boston: D. C. Heath, 1927.

Hall, Robert A. *Applied Linguistics: Italian*. S. Belasco, general editor. D. C. Heath, 1961.

Halliday, M. A. K. *The Linguistic Sciences and Language Teaching*. Bloomington: University of Indiana Press, 1964.

Handshin, C. H. *Modern Language Teaching*. Yonkers-on-Hudson: World Book, 1940. Also Handshin, C. H. *Modern Language Teaching in the United States*, Yonkers-on-Hudson; World Book, 1923.

Hanzeli, Victor E. "Foreign Language Teachers and the 'New Student': A Review Article," *MLJ* 55, no. 1 (January 1971).

————. "Linguistics and the Language Teacher." *FLA* 2, no. 1 (October 1968).

————, and Love, William D. "From Individualized Instruction to Individualized Learning." *FLA* 5, no. 3 (March 1972).

————, eds. *New Teachers for New Students.* (Proceedings of the Seattle Symposium on the Training of Foreign Language Teachers, 1970.) Available from the Modern Language Association Materials Center, 62 Fifth Avenue, New York, N. Y. 10011.

Harris, Albert J. *How to Increase Reading Ability.* New York: David McKay, 1970. Fifth Edition.

Harris, Lyndon. "The Teaching of Swahili." *MLJ* 52, no. 3 (March 1968).

Hayes, Alfred S. *Technical Guide for the Selection, Purchase, Use and Maintenance of Language Laboratory Facilities.* U. S. Office of Education, Bulletin No. 37, OE-21024, Washington, D. C.: U. S. Government Printing Office, 1963. 50¢.

Herick, Michael, and Kennedy, Dora. "Multi-Level Grouping of Students in the Modern Foreign Language Program." *FLA* 2, no. 2 (December 1968).

Hocking, Elton. "Audio-Visual Learning and Foreign Languages." In Smith, George E., and Leamon, Phillip M., eds., *Effective Foreign Language Instruction in the Secondary School.* Englewood Cliffs, N. J.: Prentice-Hall, 1969.

————. "Culture, Relevance and Survival." *MLJ* 54, no. 8 (December 1970).

————. "The Laboratory in Perspective: Teachers, Strategies, Outcomes." *MLJ* 53, no. 6 (October 1969).

————. *Language Laboratory and Language Learning.* Second Edition, Monograph No. 2. Department of Audiovisual Instruction, National Education Association of the U. S., 1967. Available from DAVI, NEA, 1201 Sixteenth Street, N. W., Washington, D. C. 20036. $4.50.

————. "The Sound of Pictures." *MLJ* 52, no. 3 (March 1968).

————. "Technology in Foreign Language Teaching." *MLJ* 54, no. 2 (February 1970).

Hoetker, James. "The Limitations and Advantages of Behavioral Objectives in the Arts and Humanities: A Guest Editorial." *FLA* 3, no. 4 (May 1970).

Holton, J. S., et al. *Sound Language Teaching.* New York: University Publishers, 1961.

Holt, John. *How Children Fail.* New York: Pitman, 1964.

Hubbard, Louise J. "Modern Languages for the Racially Disadvantaged." *MLJ* 52, no. 3 (March 1968).

Huebener, Theodore. *How to Teach Foreign Languages Effectively.* Revised edition. New York: New York University Press, 1965.

————. "The New Key Is Now Off-Key." *MLJ* 47, no. 8 (December 1963).

Hutchinson, Joseph C. "The Language Laboratory . . . How Effective Is It." U. S. Office of Education, OE-277021. Washington, D. C.: U. S. Government Printing Office, 1964. 15¢.

————. *Modern Foreign Languages in the Language Laboratory.* U.S. Office of Education, Bulletin No. 23, OE-27013. Washington, D. C.: U. S. Government Printing Office, 1963. 35¢.

Jackson, David M. "A Search for Practical Means of Improving Instruction by Increasing Students' Responsibility for their own Learning in University of Illinois High School." *National Association of Secondary School Principals Bulletin* 43 (January 1959): 233–39.

————, Shoemaker, W.L., and Westmeyer, Paul. "University of Illinois High School, Urbana, Illinois, Experiments Further with Independent Study." *National Association of Secondary School Principals Bulletin* 45 (January 1961): 198–208.

Jakobovits, Leon A. *Foreign Language Learning: A Psycholingual Approach.* Rowley, Mass.: Newbury House, 1970.

————. "A Functional Approach to the Assessment of Language Skills." *Journal of English as a Second Language* (1969): 63–76.

————. "Implications of Recent Psycholinguistic Developments for the Teaching of a Second Language." *Language Learning* 18 (1969): 89–109.

————. Introduction to "Foundations of Foreign Language Teaching and Learning; Psychological Aspects." In Reichmann, Eberhard (ed.), *The Teaching of German: Problems and Method.* National Carl Schutz Association—Teaching Aid Project. Philadelphia: Winchell Company, 1970, Part II, chap. 1.

————. "Mediation Theory and the Single Stage S-R Model: Different? *Psychological Review* 78 (1966): 376–81.

————. "Motivation and Foreign Language Learning: Part A. Motivation and Learner Factors." *Report of the 1970 Northeast Conference on the Teaching of Foreign Languages,* Joseph A. Tursi, ed.

————. "Research Findings and Foreign Language Requirements in Colleges and Universities." *FLA* 2, no. 4 (May 1969).

————. "Second Language Learning and Transfer Theory: A Theoretical Assessment." *Language Learning* 19 (1969): 55–86.

————, and Miron, M. S., eds. *Readings in the Psychology of Language.* Englewood Cliffs, N. J.: Prentice-Hall, 1967.

Johnston, Marjorie C., and Keesee, Elizabeth. *Modern Foreign Languages and Your Child.* U. S. Department of Health, Education and Welfare, Bulletin No. 1964. Publication No. OE-07020, Washington, D. C.: U. S. Government Printing Office, 1964.

————, Remer, Ilo, and Sivers, Frank. *Modern Foreign Languages: A Counselor's Guide.* U. S. Department of Health, Education and Welfare, Bulletin No. 20, 1960. Washington, D. C.: U. S. Government Printing Office, 1960. OE-27004.

Jonas, Sister Ruth A., S. C. "The Twinned Classroom Approach to FLES." *MLJ* 53, no. 5 (May 1969).

Josselson, Henry. *The Russian Word Count and Frequency Analysis*. Detroit: Wayne State University Press, 1953.

Juilland, Alphonse G., and Chang-Rodriguez, E. *Frequency Dictionary of Spanish Words*. The Hague: Mouton, 1964.

Justman, Joseph, and Naas, Martin L. "The High School Achievement of Pupils Who Were and Were Not Introduced to a Foreign Language in the Elementary School." *MLJ* 40, no. 3 (March 1956).

Kant, Julia G. "Foreign Language Registrations in Institutions of Higher Education, Fall 1968." *FLA* 3, no. 2 (December 1969).

Kaulfers, Walter V. *Modern Languages for Modern Schools*. New York: McGraw-Hill, 1942.

Keating, L. Clark. "What the French Think of Us." *MLJ* 47, no. 5 (May 1963).

Keating, Raymond F. *A Study of the Effectiveness of Language Laboratories*. New York: Institute of Administrative Research, Teachers College, Columbia University, 1963.

"The Keating Report—A Symposium." *MLJ* 48, no. 3 (April 1964).

Keller, Robert J. "Toward Differentiated Instruction." *North Central Association Quarterly* 37 (Spring 1963).

Kelly, Louis G. *25 Centuries of Language Teaching*. Rowley, Mass.: Newbury House, 1969.

Keniston, Hayward. *A Standard List of Spanish Words and Idioms*. Boston: D. C. Heath, 1941.

King, Charles L. "A Decade of NDEA Language Institutes." *Hispania* 52, no. 3 (September 1969): 361–68.

Krathwohl, David R., Bloom, Benjamin S., and Masia, Bertram B. *Taxonomy of Educational Objectives. Handbook II. Affective Domain*. New York: David McKay , 1956.

Kufner, H. L. *The Grammatical Structures of English and German*. Contrastive Structure Series. Ferguson, Charles A., general editor. Chicago: University of Chicago Press, 1962.

Lado, Robert. *Language Testing*. New York: Longmans, 1961.

——. *Language Teaching. A Scientific Approach*. New York: McGraw-Hill, Inc., 1964.

——. "Language, Thought, and Memory in Language Teaching: A Thought View." *MLJ* 54, no. 8 (December 1970).

Lambert, Richard D. "Patterns of Funding of Language and Area Studies." *Journal of Asian Studies* 30 (February 1971): 399–412.

——. "Psychological Approaches to the Study of Languages: On Learning, Thinking, and Human Abilities." *MLJ* 47, no. 2 (February 1963).

Lambert, Robert J. "On Second Language Learning and Bilingualism." *MLJ* 47, no. 3 (March 1963).

Lambert, W. E., and Gardner, R. C. *Attitudes and Motivation in Second-Language Learning*. Rowley, Mass.: Newbury House, 1972.

————, Barik, H. C. and Tunstall, K. "Attitudinal and Cognitive Aspects of Intensive Study of a Second Language." *Journal of Abnormal and Social Psychology* 66 (1963).

————, and Jakobovits, Leon. "Verbal Satiation and Changes in the Intensity of Meaning." *Journal of Experimental Psychology* 60 (1960).

Landry, Joseph A. *Graded French Word and Idiom Book*. Boston: D. C. Heath, 1938.

Leavitt, Sturgess E. "The Teaching of Spanish in the United States." *Reports of Surveys and Studies in the Teaching of Modern Foreign Languages*. New York: Modern Language Association, 1961.

Lewald, Ernest H. "A Tentative Outline of Problems in the Knowledge, Understanding and Teaching of Cultures." *MLJ* 52, no. 5 (May 1968).

Lewis, Karen R. "Transformational-Generative Grammar: A New Consideration to Teaching Foreign Languages." *MLJ* 56, no. 1 (January 1972).

Linguistic Reporter. Center for Applied Linguistics, 1611 North Kent St., Arlington, Virginia 22209.

Lipton, Gladys C. "To Read or Not to Read: An Experiment in the FLES Level." *FLA* 3, no. 2 (December 1969).

"Local AAT Chapters: Their Role in the National Picture," *MLJ* 51, no. 5 (May 1967).

Lumsdaine, A. A., and Glaser, Robert. *Teaching Machines and Programmed Learning: A Source Book*. National Education Association, Department of Audio-Visual Instruction, 1960.

MacAllister, Archibald T. "The Preparation of College Teachers of Modern Foreign Languages." *PMLA* 79, no. 2 (May 1964).

Macirone, T. *Practical French Phonetics*. Allyn and Bacon, 1921.

Mackey, William F. *Language Teaching Analysis*. Bloomington: University of Indiana Press, 1965.

Magner, Thomas. *Applied Linguistics: Russian*. Edited by S. Belasco. Boston: D. C. Heath, 1961.

Manlove, Donald C. and Beggs, David W., III. *Flexible Scheduling Using the IndiFlexS Model*. Bold New Venture Series. Bloomington and London: Indiana University Press, 1965.

Marchand, James W. *Applied Linguistics: German*. Edited by S. Belasco. Boston: D. C. Heath, 1961.

Marty, Fernand. *Language Laboratory Learning*. Wellesley: Visual Publications, 1960.

Mathieu, Gustave. *Advances in the Teaching of Modern Languages*, vol. 2. Oxford: Pergamon Press, 1966.

————. "Pitfalls of Pattern Practice: An Exegesis." *MLJ* 48, no. 1 (January 1964).

Mayer, Robert F. *Preparing Objectives for Programmed Instruction*. San Francisco: Fearon, 1962.

McDavid, Raven I., Jr. "Mencken Revisited." *Harvard Educational Review* 34, no. 2 (Spring 1964).

Meiden, Walter, and Murphy, Joseph A. "The Use of the Language Laboratory to Teach the Reading Lesson." *MLJ* 52, no. 1 (January 1968).

Michel, Joseph. *Foreign Language Teaching*. New York: Macmillan, 1967.

Mildenberger, Kenneth W., ed. *MLA Guide to Federal Programs*. New York: MLA/ERIC, 62 Fifth Avenue, New York 10011, 1969.

Ministère de l'Education Nationale. *Le Français Fondamental (Premier Degré)*. Philadelphia: Chilton, 1954.

Modern Foreign Languages, a Six-Year Program (Grades 7-12): French, German, Spanish. Raleigh, North Carolina: State Board of Education, 1963. ERIC Document No. Ed-013581.

Modern Language Association Foreign Language Proficiency Tests for Teachers and Advanced Students. Educational Testing Service, Princeton, N. J. 08540, 1961. A seven-battery test including areas on listening comprehension, speaking, reading, writing, applied linguistics, civilization and culture, and professional preparation. The battery is available in five languages: French, German, Italian, Russian, and Spanish. Different forms available in each language. Write Educational Testing Service for a description. A 38-page booklet is distributed free of charge.

Modern Language Association. *Reports of Surveys and Studies in the Teaching of Modern Foreign Languages*. New York: Modern Language Association, 1961.

Modern Language Project for the Public Schools of Boston, Mass., 1961. *Parlons Français* Series. Heath de Rochmont.

Modern Language Teaching by Television. Council for Cultural Cooperation of the Council of Europe. Strasbourg, 1965.

Moore, Michael J. "The Articulation Jungle." *The French Review* 44, no. 2 (December 1970).

Morain, Genelle. "Teaching for Cross-Cultural Understanding: An Annotated Bibliography." *FLA* 5, no. 1 (October 1971).

Morgan, Bayard Q. *German Frequency Word Book*. New York: Macmillan, 1928.

Moskowitz, Gertrude. "The Effects of Training Foreign Language Teachers in Interaction Analysis." *FLA* 1, no. 3 (March 1968).

————. "Interaction Analysis: A New Modern Language for Supervisors." *FLA* 5, no. 2 (December 1971).

Moulton, William G. "Applied Linguistics in the Classroom." *PMLA* 76 (May 1961).

————. *The Sounds of English and German.* Contrastive Structure Series. Ferguson, Charles A., general editor. Chicago: University of Chicago Press, 1962.

National Society for the Study of Education. *Individualizing Instruction.* Sixty-first Yearbook of the Society, Part 1. Chicago: University of Chicago Press, 1962.

Norman, Donald A. *Memory and Attention.* New York: Wiley and Sons, 1969.

Northeast Conference on the Teaching of Foreign Languages. See Appendix A.

Nostrand, Howard Lee. "Language, Culture and the Curriculum." In Donoghue, Mildred R., ed., *Foreign Languages and the Schools.* Dubuque: William C. Brown, 1967.

————, et al. *Research on Language Teaching: An Annotated Bibliography for 1945-1964.* Second revised edition. Seattle: University of Washington Press, 1964.

Nuttal, Ronald L. "The Effect of a Tracking System of Student Satisfaction and Achievement." *American Educational Research Journal* 8, no. 3 (May 1971).

Oliva, Peter F. *The Teaching of Foreign Languages.* Englewood Cliffs, N. J.: Prentice-Hall, Inc., 1969.

Olivero, James L. "The Meaning and Application of Differentiated Staffing in Teaching." *Phi Delta Kappan* (September 1970).

————, and Buffie, Edward G., eds. *Educational Manpower: From Aides to Differentiated Staff Patterns.* Bold New Ventures Series. Bloomington and London: Indiana University Press, 1970.

Oller, John W., Jr. "Transformational Theory and Pragmatics." *MLJ* 54, no. 7 (November 1970).

Olsen, Paul. *Reality and Relevance: Yearbook, 1969.* Washington: The American Association of Colleges for Teacher Education, 1969.

O'Neill, William F., ed. *Selected Educational Heresies.* Chicago: Scott, Foresman, 1969.

Ornstein, Jacob. "Programmed Instruction and Educational Technology in the Language Field." *MLJ* 52, no. 7 (November 1968).

O'Rourke, Everett V. "Continuum in Language Learning." In Mathieu, Gustave, ed., *Advances in the Teaching of Modern Languages.* Vol. II. Oxford: Pergamon Press, 1966. Chapter 11.

Paine, Doris T. "Who's to Teach My Child Foreign Language?" *MLJ* 41, no. 4 (April 1962).

Papalia, Anthony. "A Study of Attrition in Foreign Language Enrollments in Four Suburban Public Schools." *FLA* 4, no. 1 (October 1970).

————, and Zampogna, Joseph. "An Experiment in Individualized Instruction through Small Group Interaction." *FLA* 5, no. 3 (March 1972).

Parker, William Riley. *The National Interest and Foreign Languages*, 3rd Ed. U. S. Department of State Publication No. 7324. Washington, D. C., 1962.

———. "What's Past Is Prologue." *PMLA* 71, no. 2 (April 1956).

Parry, Albert. *America Learns Russian*. Syracuse: Syracuse University Press, 1967.

Paulston, Christina Bratt. "Structural Pattern Drills: A Classification." *FLA* 4, no. 2 (December 1970).

Pei, Mario. *Glossary of Linguistic Terminology*. New York: Doubleday, 1966.

Penfield, Wilder G. *Speech and Brain Mechanisms*. Princeton: Princeton University Press, 1959.

Perkins, Jean A. "State Certification and Proficiency Tests: The Experience in Pennsylvania." *FLA* 2, no. 2 (December 1968).

Pfeffer, J. Alan. *Grunddeutsch. Basic [Spoken] German Word List. Grundstufe.* Englewood Cliffs, N. J.: Prentice-Hall, 1964.

Pillet, Roger A. "Demands of New Dimensions." *The School Review* 73, no. 2 (Summer 1965).

———. "French with Slides and Tapes—A Reappraisal." *Elementary School Journal* 65, no. 2 (November 1964).

———. "The Impact of FLES: An Appraisal." *MLJ* 52, no. 8 (December 1968).

———. "Individualizing Instruction: Implications for FLES Bulletins of the Department of Foreign Language." *NEA* 5, no. 2 (December 1967).

———. "Prospects for FLES." In Mathieu, Gustave, ed., *Advances in the Teaching of Modern Languages*. Oxford: Pergamon Press, 1966: pp. 196–210.

———. "Selected References on Elementary School Instruction: Foreign Languages." *Elementary School Journal* 60 (1959).

———. "Selected References on Elementary School Instruction: Foreign Languages." *Elementary School Journal* 61 (1960): 104–7.

———. "Selected References on Elementary School Instruction: Foreign Languages." *Elementary School Journal* 62, no. 2 (1961): 102–6.

———. "Selected References on Elementary School Instruction: Foreign Languages." *Elementary School Journal* 64, no. 2 (1963): 102–3.

———. "Teacher Training in Foreign Languages: An Overview." *MLJ* 54, no. 1 (January 1970).

———, and Garrabrant, F. "French with Slides and Tapes." *Elementary School Journal* 62, no. 8 (May 1962).

The Pimsleur Language Aptitude Battery, 1966. Harcourt Brace Jovanovich, 757 Third Avenue, New York, New York 10017.

Pimsleur, Paul. *Foreign Language Proficiency Tests*. Harcourt, Brace and World, 1967. Achievement tests in three languages: French, German, and Spanish. For the first three levels of language study. Separate tests measure proficiency in listening (test 1), speaking (test 2), reading (test 3), and writing skills (test 4). Price and description information available from publisher.

————. "A Memory Schedule." *MLJ* 51, no. 2 (February 1967).

————. *Psychological experiments related to second language learning: Report of the NDEA conference.* Los Angeles: University of California Press, 1959.

————, and Bonkowski, R. G. "The Transfer of Verbal Material across Sense Modalities." *Journal of Educational Psychology* 52 (1961).

————, and Quinn, Terence, eds. *The Psychology of Second Language Learning.* New York: Cambridge University Press, 1971.

————, Sundland, D. M., and McIntyre, Ruth D. "Underachievement in Foreign Language Learning." *International Review of Applied Linguistics* 2 (1964).

Politzer, Robert L. *Characteristics and Behaviors of the Successful Foreign Language Teacher, 1969.* Philadelphia: Chilton, 1972.

————. *An Experiment in Improving Achievement in Foreign Language through Learning of Selected Skills Associated with Language Aptitude, 1969.* Philadelphia: Chilton, 1972.

————. "The Impact of Linguistics on Language Teaching: Past, Present and Future." *MLJ* 48 (March 1965).

————. *Language Learning, A Linguistic Introduction.* Englewood Cliffs, New Jersey: Prentice-Hall, 1965, 1970.

————. *Linguistics and Applied Linguistics: Aims and Methods.* Philadelphia, Pa.: Center for Curriculum Development, Inc., 1972.

————. "On the Relation of Linguistics to Language Teaching." *MLJ* 42, no. 2 (February 1958).

————. "On the Use of Aptitude Variables in Research in Teaching." *International Review of Applied Linguistics* 8, no. 4 (November 1970): 333–40.

————. "Some Reflections on Pattern Practice." *MLJ* 48, no. 1 (January 1964).

————. "Student Motivation and Interest in Elementary Language Courses." *Language Learning* 5 (1953-54).

————. *Teaching French.* Boston: Ginn and Co., 1960.

————. *Teaching German.* Wallhorn: Blaisdell, 1968.

————. *Teaching Spanish.* Boston: Ginn and Co., 1961.

————. "Toward Individualization in Foreign Language Teaching." *MLJ* 55, no. 4 (April 1971).

Poston, Laurence. "William Riley Parker (1906-1968)." *Hispania* 52, no. 3 (September 1969): 355-56.

Preller, Arno G. "Some Problems Involved in Compiling Word Frequency Lists," *MLJ* 54, no. 5 (May 1970).

Prince, Roy J. "An Institute Director Looks Back." *Hispania* 52, no. 3 (September 1969): 368–75.

"Qualifications for Secondary School Teachers of Modern Foreign Languages." *Bulletin of National Association of Secondary School Principals* 39, no. 214 (November 1955): 30–33. Reprinted in *MLJ*, golden anniversary issue, 50, no. 6 (October 1966), Appendix B.

"Qualifications for Teachers of Modern Foreign Language." *PMLA* 77, no. 4, Part 2 (September 1962): 38. Reprinted in Andersson, Theodore. *Foreign Languages in the Elementary School.* Austin: University of Texas Press (1969): 38–39.

Rallo, John A. "A Cooperative French Program: A New Approach." *FLA* 2, no. 4 (May 1969).

Randall, Earle S. "Research in Three Large Televised FLES Programs." Modern Language Association FLES Packet, New York, *MLA* (1967). Discontinued.

Remer, Ilo. *Handbook for Guiding Students in Modern Foreign Languages.* U. S. Department of Health, Education and Welfare, Bulletin no. 26, 1963. Washington: U. S. Government Printing Office, 1963, OE-77018.

Reinert, Harry. "Student Attitudes toward Foreign Language—No Sale!" *MLJ* 54, no. 2 (February 1970).

Report of the Bloomington Conference, 1969. *Guidelines for Three Levels of Competence in French.* State of Illinois, Superintendent of Public Instruction, Springfield, Illinois.

Reports of the FLES Committee of the AATF, 1961-1970. See Appendix B.

Rivers, Wilga. *The Psychologist and the Foreign-Language Teacher.* Chicago: University of Chicago Press, 1964.

———. *Teaching Foreign-Language Skills.* Chicago: University of Chicago Press, 1968.

———. *Speaking in Many Tongues: Essays in Foreign-Language Teaching.* Rowley, Mass.: Newbury House, 1972.

Roeming, Robert F. "The Contributing of the Classroom Teacher to Research and Knowledge." *FLA* 1, no. 1 (October 1967).

Rosenbaum, Peter S. "The Computer as a Learning Environment for Foreign Language Instruction." *FLA* 2, no. 4 (May 1969).

Russo, Ben J. *Curriculum Articulation in Foreign Languages, Grades Four through Twelve.* Portage, Wisconsin: Portage Senior High School. ERIC Document No. FL 000-288.

Sacks, Norman P. "Some Aspects of the Application of Linguistics to the Teaching of Modern Foreign Languages." *MLJ* 48, no. 1 (January 1964).

———. "Training the New College Instructor." *MLJ* 50, no. 6 (October 1966).

Saviano, Eugene. "Wichita State University's Involvement in the NDEA Institute Program." *Hispania* 52, no. 3 (September 1969): 375–83.

Scanlan, Richard T. "Computer-Assisted Instruction: PLATO in Latin." *FLA* 5, no. 1 (October 1971).

Scherer, George, and Wertheimer, Michael. *A Psycholinguistic Experiment in Foreign Language Teaching.* New York: McGraw-Hill, 1964.

Seelye, H. Ned. "Culture in Foreign Language Classroom." *Illinois Journal of Education* 59, no. 3 (March 1968).

———. "Performance Objectives for Teaching Cultural Concepts." *FLA* 3, no. 4 (May 1970).

Seidel, Edwin H. "The Teaching of German in the United States from Colonial Times to the Present." *Reports of Surveys and Studies in the Teaching of Modern Foreign Languages.* New York: Modern Language Association, 1961.

Sherif, June L. *Handbook of Foreign Language Occupations.* New York: Regents Publishing Co., 1966.

Short, Edmund C., and Marconnit, George D. *Contemporary Thought on Public School Curriculum: Readings.* Dubuque, Iowa: William C. Brown, 1968.

Shulman, Lee S. "Perspectives on the Psychology of Learning and the Teaching of Science and Mathematics." Address to the American Association for the Advancement of Science, New York City, December 1967.

Shuman, R. Baird. "Let's Get Foreign Language Teachers Out of Our Public High Schools!" *MLJ* 55, no. 1 (January 1971).

Skinner, B. F. "The Science of Learning and the Art of Teaching." *Harvard Educational Review* 24 (1954).

Smith, B.O., and others. *Teachers for the Real World.* Washington: American Association of Colleges for Teacher Education, 1969.

Smith, Bardwell L. "Educational Trends and the Seventies." *AAUP Bulletin* 56, no. 2 (June 1970).

Smith, Philip D., Jr. and others. *A Comparison Study of the Effectiveness of the Traditional Audio-Lingual Laboratory Equipment.* Washington: U. S. Department of Health, Education and Welfare, 1969.

Spaar, Virginia. "FLES in Retrospect." In "The FLES Student, A Study." Report of the FLES Committee of the American Association of Teachers of French, December 1967, Miami, Florida. Pp. 97–124.

Spencer, Richard E., and Glaugher, Ronald L. "A Study of an Assumption about High School and College Equivalency in Language Training." *MLJ* 51, no. 6 (October 1967).

Stabler, E., ed. *The Education of the Secondary School Teacher.* Wesleyan University Press, 1962.

Stack, Edward M. *The Language Laboratory and Modern Language Teaching.* Revised edition. New York: Oxford University Press, 1966.

Steiner, Florence. "Individualized Instruction." *MLJ* 55, no. 6 (October 1971).

———. "Performance Objectives in the Teaching of Foreign Languages." *FLA* 3, no. 4 (May 1970).

———. "Teaching Literature by Performance Objectives." *FLA* 5, no. 3 (March 1972).

Stern, H. H. "First and Second Language Acquisition." *Perspectives on Second Language Teaching.* Ontario: Modern Language Center Publications, No. 1, 1970.

Stewart, George R. *Names on the Land*. Boston: Houghton Mifflin, 1958.

Stockwell, R. P., and Bowen, J. D. *The Grammatical Structure of English and Spanish*. The Contrastive Structure Series. Ferguson, Charles A., general editor. Chicago: University of Chicago Press, 1965.

————. *The Sounds of English and Spanish*. Contrastive Structure Series. Ferguson, Charles A., general editor. Chicago: University of Chicago Press, 1965.

Strasheim, Lorraine A. "The Anvil or the Hammer: A Guest Editorial." *FLA* 4, no. 1 (October 1970).

Sullivan, M. W. "Programmed Learning in Foreign Languages." In Calvin, Allen D., ed., *Programmed Instruction: Bold New Venture*. Bold New Venture Series. Bloomington and London: Indiana University Press, 1969.

Suppes, Patrick, and Jerman, Max. "Computer-Assisted Instruction." *National Association of Secondary School Principals Bulletin* 54, 343 (1970): 27–40.

Sweet, Phyllis R., and Nuttall, Ronald. "The Effects of a Tracking System on Student Satisfaction and Achievement." *American Education Research Journal* 8, no. 3 (May 1971).

Swenson, Rodney. *A Frequency Count of Contemporary German Vocabulary Based on Three Current Leading Newspapers*. Final Report. Minneapolis: University of Minnesota, 1967. OE Contract No. 3-7-068838-1576.

"Teacher Preparation for FLES." *MLJ* 50, no. 6 (October 1966): 95–99. Appendix N.

"Ten Years of NDEA Language Institutes (1959-1968): Four Perspectives and a Memorial to the Architect." *Hispania* 52, no. 3 (September 1969): 357–83.

Terwillinger, Ronald I. "Multi-grade Proficiency Group: Grouping for Foreign Language Instruction." *MLJ* 54, no. 5 (May 1970).

Thelen, Herbert A. *Classroom Grouping for Teachability*. New York: Wiley, 1967.

————. *Education and the Human Quest*. New York: Harper, 1960.

Trump, J. Lloyd. *New Directions to Quality Education*. Washington: National Association of Secondary School Principals, 1956.

Tyler, Ralph, Gagné, Robert, and Scriven, Michael. *Perspectives of Curriculum Evaluation*. American Educational Research Association Monograph Series on Curriculum Evaluation. American Educational Research Association, Washington, D. C., 1967.

Vakar, Nicholas P. *A Word Count of Spoken Russian: The Soviet Usage*. Columbus: Ohio State University Press, 1966.

Valdman, Albert. *Applied Linguistics: French*. Edited by S. Belasco. Boston: D. C. Heath, 1961.

————. The implementation and evaluation of a multiple-credit self-instructional elementary French course. Indiana University, 1965. Multilith.

————. "From Structural Analysis to Pattern Drill." *French Review* 34 (December 1960).

————. "Toward a Better Implementation of the Audio-Lingual Approach." *MLJ* 54, no. 5 (May 1970).

————, ed. *Trends in Language Teaching.* New York: McGraw-Hill, 1966.

Valette, Rebecca M. "Laboratory Quizzes: A Means of Increasing Laboratory Effectiveness." *FLA* 1, no. 1 (October 1967).

————. *Modern Language Testing: A Handbook.* New York: Harcourt, Brace and World, 1967. Available from the publisher. $4.75.

————, and Disick, Renee S. *Modern Language Performance Objectives and Individualization.* New York: Harcourt Brace Jovanovich, Inc., 1972.

Vander Beke, George E. *French Word Book.* New York: Macmillan, 1929.

Van Eenenaam, Evelyn. "Annotated Bibliography of Modern Language Methodology for 1957." *MLJ* 43, no. 1 (January 1959).

————. "Annotated Bibliography of Modern Language Methodology for 1958." *MLJ* 44, no. 1 (January 1960).

————. "Annotated Bibliography of Modern Language Methodology for 1959." *MLJ* 45, no. 1 (January 1961).

Vocalo, Joseph M. "The Effect of Foreign Language Study in the Elementary School upon Achievement in the Same Foreign Language in the High School." *MLJ* 51, no. 8 (December 1967).

Walton, Wesley W. "Computers in the Classroom: Master or Servant?" *National Association of Secondary School Principals Bulletin* 54, 343 (1970): 9–17.

Wasserman, Marvin, ed. *Proceedings: Thirty-second Annual Foreign Language Conference at New York University.* New York University School of Education, Department of Foreign Languages and Internation Relations Education, 1966.

Watson, Goodwin. *What Psychology Can We Trust?* Bureau of Publications, Teachers College, Columbia University, 1961.

Watts, George B. "The Teaching of French in the United States: A History." *French Review* 37, No. 1 (October 1963).

West, Michael P. *The Construction of Reading Material for Teaching a Foreign Language.* London: Oxford University Press, 1927.

————. *Learning to Read Foreign Languages.* London: Longmans Green and Co., 1926.

Whang, Young Kyu. *The Interaction of Short-Term Memory and Instructional Variables on Verbal Activity.* Unpublished Ph.D. dissertation, Department of Education, University of Chicago, 1971.

Willbern, Glen. "Foreign Language Enrollments in Public Secondary Schools, 1965." *FLA* 1, no. 3 (March 1968).

————. "Foreign Language Entrance and Degree Requirements in Colleges That Grant the B. A. Degree: Fall, 1966." *FLA* 1, no. 1 (October 1967).

Williams, Gloria W. "Pitfalls in Teaching Foreign Languages." *Chicago Schools Journal* 42 (October 1960).

Wolf, W. C. "Knowledge Generation." *Educational Researcher* (January 1970).

Wood, Fred H. "The McCluer Plan: Innovative Non-Graded Foreign Language Program." *MLJ* 54, no. 3 (March 1970).

Wragg, E. C. "Interaction Analysis in the Foreign Language Classroom." *MLJ* 54, no. 2 (February 1970).

Zeldner, Max. "The Bewildered Modern Language Teacher." *MLJ* 47, no.6 (October 1963).

Ziegler, Rosario B. "On Starting a FLES Program." *Hispania* 46 (March 1963): 144–45.

Index